THIS SIDE
OF
ANYWHERE

Minnesota
Farm
Chronicles

Vivian Norberg
Loken

A church bell echoes through this
memoir and a stream chatters.

EAGLE EDITIONS
2004

EAGLE EDITIONS
AN IMPRINT OF HERITAGE BOOKS, INC.

Books, CDs, and more—Worldwide

For our listing of thousands of titles see our website
at
www.HeritageBooks.com

Published 2004 by
HERITAGE BOOKS, INC.
Publishing Division
1540 Pointer Ridge Place #E
Bowie, Maryland 20716

International Standard Book Number: 0-7884-2531-5

Table of Contents

I.   INTRODUCTION

1).   Introduction
       By boat, by train, on foot he traveled here,
       Olaf - - a brave and hardy pioneer.

2.)   The New Country
       The man from Sweden strode through wilderness,
       To find the home site he asked God to bless.

3.)   The Land
       The sounds and smells and textures lured me on,
       To more adventure than I had ever known.

4.)   The Fire
       Sun-baked were the forests, fields, and plains,
       A tinderbox for sparks from passing trains.

5.)   The River
       The waters sang and chattered as they flowed
       Along where ghosts of other centuries rode.

II.   ABOUT OUR LIVES AND TIMES

6.)   The Bridge
       Nature challenged man's display of might.
       She flung her ice chunks at the bridge both day and
       night.

7.)   The Cooperative
       When the pasture-grass stood tall and rich and
        green,
       The milk we sold was richer than we'd ever seen.

8.)   The Coompa
       Some would say our meal was 'peasants fare',
       But our concern was that we got our share.

9.) The Pressed Meat
   With care we took the cover off and looked,
   Into the boiler where the hog's head cooked.

10.) The Rummegrot
   Some thought this was the richest kind of fare,
   The choicest (if you liked it) anywhere.

11.) The Fever
   Our neighbors and our kinfolk stayed away,
   The risk of 'catching it' too high a price to pay.

12.) The Mortgage
   We lived in haunted houses, you might say,
   The ghost foreclosure lurked along the way.

13.) The Threshers
   I missed the whispers of the stalks of grain,
   That caught the language of the wind and rain.

14.) The Rights Of Women
   My Mother ventured bravely down the road;
   It was her 'first-time-driving' episode.

15.) The Washday
   Washing our clothes required endless time;
   We scrubbed away all traces of the grime.

16.) The Neighbors
   I followed the ruts, that marked the bumpy way,
   Up to the neighbor's farm place, on that day.

III. THE FARM HOUSE

17.) The House
   Two stories high, the house looked to the west.
   Too modest to lay claim to being 'best.'

18.) The Teakettle
A smoldering fire in the stove would be
Enough to keep the kettle bubbling cheerfully.

19.) The Kitchen Range
Just a chunk of metal, you might say,
But it kept the embers glowing night and day.

20.) The Claw-Legged Kitchen Table
We gathered there together every day,
To eat, and play and sometimes talk, and pray.

21.) The Chimney Corner Spy
All traffic through the household passed me by;
I was the shameless chimney corner spy.

22.) The Pantry
The tastiest of foods found refuge there,
Secure unless we sampled on a dare.

23.) The Quilt
Across the length and breadth of that percale,
Acres of flowers bloomed - - as in a fairy tale.

24.) The Radio
On currents of the frost-encrusted air,
A wave of spirit-richness met me there.

25.) The Christmas Cactus
Framed by a window looking south and east,
The cactus, blooming, was a visual feast.

26.) The Room
A host of memories stretch and loiter there
And rock the years away in that old chair.

27.) The Heating Stove
My fingers on the firebox could feel,
Its ice-cold trim above a field of steel.

28.) The Lamps
When, rosy heeled, the sun moved out of sight,
Our lamps provided us with pools of light.

29.) The Newspapers
Stacks of papers strewn across the floor - -
How could a reading family ask for more?

IV. ABOUT OUR YARD

30.) The Extravaganza
They flashed around us every summer night;
Those glow worms, tracing patterns in their flight.

31.) The Granary
Dust motes danced along in beams of light,
That streamed through every spider web in sight.

32.) The Spokesman
Before the morning's light, his clarion call
Had pierced the deepest dreams of one and all.

33.) The Lilacs
I was surprised again year after year,
To see the fragrant blossoms reappear.

34.) The Pansy Bed
From the kitchen window she could see,
Their pansy faces, dipping flippantly.

35.) The Poplar Grove
With every romping breeze that came to play,
The poplar leaves spun briskly night or day.

36.) The Pine Tree
Towering above us, that pine tree,
Stood in our yard for half a century.

37.) The Dumping Ground
Today's belongings are tomorrow's trash,
Will usefulness and fond attachment clash?

IV.   ABOUT OUR ACREAGE

38.)   The Fence Posts
They strutted by the roadside, up and down,
Some heading north and others toward the town.

39.)   The Old Barn
In stanchions side-by-side the cattle stood;
The milk they gave was for our livelihood.

40.)   The Choice
My choice of breed is bound to be the best,
It will put your make or model to the test.

41.)   The Garden
The garden is a sundial, if you read it right,
Its shifting shadows tell you when the day us taking
Flight.

42.)   The Repairman
With best of intentions and a willing hand,
Papa *impaired* machinery in his command.

43.)   The Bull Calf
"Be kind to beasts," I've heard the righteous say,
But patience ran behind its limits on that day.

44.)   Epilogue
We've reached the final chapter now, and I
will leave you here to read. This is 'goodbye'.

This book is dedicated to my family, who share my heritage, to my special helpers, and to my faithful group.

I could not have done this without all of the prayers, and the supporters who helped me believe in myself.

Thanks to those who gave me their time and talents to make the book possible; thanks to Judy J., to Jan H. and to Erik Paul.

FOREWORD

"For they conquer who believe they can."

A Roman poet made the above comment centuries ago. I believe it is a timeless and universal truth. Examples exist in every society all around the earth..

As I wrote about Grandfather Olaf, I came to feel closer to him. I found a voice for him that seemed to fit his personage.

That voice takes another form in the bell of the church that Grandfather Olaf helped to build adjacent to our farm property. It fills my memory, sometimes riding high above, at other times tolling quietly around me. Always reminding me that faith brought Grandfather Olaf here.

I hold his example before me. When I'm in the grip of negatives, I ask for God's help in conquering them. I believe Grandfather Olaf did that, too.

Without a doubt, Grandfather Olaf had faults. But, still, he acted on his wish to come to America and, further, made a good and prosperous matter of this monumental decision. I see Grandfather Olaf as a conqueror.

§§§

one

INTRODUCTION

By boat, by train, on foot he traveled here,
Olaf - - a brave and hardy pioneer.

Grandfather Olaf Norberg came to Mora, Minnesota in 1882. County records show that he was the third person to take land in Northern Kanabec County and that he applied for a homestead claim in 1883, the same year Mora became a village. His directions to the place from Mora were to follow the Knife River to his home site.

He told his wife, Anna, back in Nasviken (Angsagen), Sweden, "The place I chose for our own has many trees. There are flat places for planting crops, and a river running through it to water the livestock." What did Anna say? Maybe she thought Olaf was just telling big stories. Maybe she wondered how much to believe.

That place Olaf claimed became my home. He picked the site for a dwelling and built a log cabin. It was small but it would shelter them for the time being.

He cleared the land for the building site, knowing that he would also need to house his livestock during winter months.

Plans included room for a barn and other buildings.

The buildings fronted the property, with the land broken for fields stretching eastward toward the river. When he could manage it, he built fences around his acreage.

Olaf and Anna came as pioneers. I wonder if they had any idea how much the world was changing?

One of Olaf's early concerns was to provide protection for animals. In time, he built a chicken house, granary, barn and machine shed.

The house they moved into from the log cabin came much later. At that time, they would have been astonished to learn that he would build a second house on the same foundation. That is the house I knew as a home.

It met our needs as a family. When we dined in the dining room that he had planned and built, we sat at the same table he had provided.

Grandfather Olaf's blueprints which may have been called something different - - included dimensions for a generous-sized kitchen. Three kitchen windows framed a passage toward the setting sun. It seemed to me like a fairy tale pathway to the Land of Tomorrow.

In the living room of the house, under the watchful eyes of Grandfather Olaf and Grandmother Anna Stina from their portraits on the wall, we lifted our voices and sang praises to God. Guided by the organ's music we sang the same hymns as those pouring forth from the church that Grandfather Olaf dreamed from its foundation. In that setting, we wove our own family traditions.

I looked from an upstairs window during summertime and admired the acres of fragrant clover bending obediently to the wind. In the wintertime, I saw the same fields with a snow covering that was pushed by the winds into sculptured drifts.

At first, much of Olaf's time was spent clearing away the brush and picking rocks. Later, he would turn the sod, till the earth and plant crops.

2

The fields stretching eastward provided hay and grain. Fertility of the land amazed Olaf, and he had more acreage than he ever dreamed of owning.

Grandfather Olaf died before I was born. He was never to know the homesteaded land was dear to me. That I walked along the river and wondered if sometimes I walked in his very footsteps.

I reveled in the marshy places at riverside where dragonflies darted in and out like exclamation points with gauzy wings.

Even during winter months the river attracted me. I heard the music of the stream, for I had memorized every note.

In time to come, I would stand at an upstairs window and admire the sight below. Fields covered with snow offered a dazzling view. When a glaze of moisture covered them, the surface caught the sun's rays in a blaze of brilliance.

Later, a radio came to rest on a table in the dining room of the house that Olaf built. We learned that the world was changing, and we were invited to change along with it.

What a challenge!

At last, Olaf and Anna came to the place where they could devote their time to efforts beyond bare necessities.

A farm with dairy cattle began to take shape. They had chickens and perhaps ducks and geese. Horses replaced the oxen. A piece of cleared earth became a garden.

Olaf and Anna became citizens of America. where many of their dreams were fulfilled.

Across the front of the house, a porch smiled its hospitality for another half century. But now, strangers pull shades over the windows at night.

Strangers listen in summer from the back door to the music of crickets and the low hum of the river. Strangers now take one last look before closing up the house to see if the Northern Lights are active.

The house that Olaf built has a hallowed place in memory.

Grandfather Olaf and Grandmother Anna did not know the changes that were in the offing. Those changes took place at a rapid rate. Their reality creates a need for this book which allows the contrast between then and now. I offer you scenes from my Writer's Sketchbook.

§§§

two

THE NEW COUNTRY

The man from Sweden strode through wilderness,
To find the home site that his God would bless.

I walked near the Knife River, which flows a
few miles south of Knife Lake. And the latter
wears its fame modestly as if too much
mention were already made of the early French
explorers and their visits to local Indian tribes at this
place. The journals of Pierre Esprit Radisson make
mention of a meeting at this locale, the purpose of
which was to trade such things as knives, (hence Knife
River and Knife Lake) hatchets, brass rings, and awls
for furs, especially beaver.

What a wonderful exchange of jargon must have
taken place. The correct French from Radisson. The
uneven, but equally interesting Indian dialects. The
excited explanations of interpreters. All of it
interspersed with the language of the water. The
constantly rippling movement of Knife River. This very
place where I was standing had seen and heard it all.

The smell of decayed leaves strewn at the
water's edge made me feel good. Water splashing
around rocks freshened the air. Its welcome aroma
teasing my senses.

As I followed the river, bringing the cows home
to be milked, I felt as if I'd traveled far away. The bell
fastened around the neck of the lead cow in the herd
tinkled softly from a distance. It was like an echo of

the bell in the steeple of the church Grandfather Olaf helped to found on the northern edge of our farm.

This was the river that Grandfather Olaf discovered as he walked here for the first time - - the river that probably sounded too good to be true to Grandmother Anna. The same river that swelled when snow melted in spring and after heavy rainfall. The same river that slowed to a chattery stream during long dry spells. It was always chipper-sounding like a happy-go-lucky-man who tips his hat, and smiles at all whom he meets. At the place where it curved east and south the river looked like a watery, rock-bound elbow.

At the western limits of his land, Olaf built a log cabin in which they lived at the beginning. As soon as possible, he built a house. It was like a palace to them. A grand home here in America.

For a long time after I had returned from the area of the river, I still heard its music.

Sometimes, standing in our yard, I stopped to listen for the rush of water. If I paid careful attention, I could hear its tones, like chords we found on the organ - - the water splashing over the rocks. The water licking the feet of millions of little stones.

These facts were of particular interest to me. I knew that if I were to dig around beside the river, I would no doubt turn up arrow heads. While some would be of a later date, others might be traced back to that early period during which explorers and tribesmen conducted business here.

As I walked along, a noticeable splash in the river meant activity from the beaver that built a dam right along the curve beside me. I could see a network of tree branches piled up. The river, at this point, ran deeply enough to hold the dam. A telltale splat gave proof of the beaver's tail striking water.

I noticed but went on as I listened for the whine of wind through trees with unevenly spaced and scanty branches. And, so, the wind ran through its range of sounds. I went on, satisfied, having found what I came for.

Focused as I was I jumped when a grouse flew out of its hiding place with a loud drumming noise. So stealthily the bird moves that I never saw him fly away. The drumming sound through the dense undergrowth meant he was signaling a possible mate.

My footsteps stopped at the sound of a train whistle from its location roughly two miles away. In the clear air, I could hear the wheels rumbling over the tracks. The sound moved on and always farther on, until at last it outdistanced my hearing.

Past the curve of the river, the terrain of the land rolled softly. In a certain spot, I cupped my hands around my mouth and called, "Here I am!" My skin prickled when the echo came back to me. "Here I am!" I had found my invisible playmate.

I turned to make my way back home. Although at mid-day the dairy herd grazed in the pastureland, I walked by habit along the lane where the cattle followed the bell cow so regularly you could almost set your clock by their appearance.

I followed along the barbed-wire fence. We all had respect for the barbed wire. I had plenty of scratches and welts on my arms and legs to testify to the sharpness of the barbs. Sometimes the cows rubbed against the fence as they vied for a certain place in the lane. They came away after such skirmishes with bleeding gouges in their flesh.

Right now, the lane was free and clear. I wondered if Thor, our horse, would catch up with me. A king of sensations, he often came thundering down the lane as if to prove his supremacy. At such times, he tossed his mane in a regal manner, whinnied loudly and pawed the dirt in a cloud of dust.

Now I was nearing the farmstead. I ran my hand over smooth bark of birch trees along outer limits of our yard. That produced an adventure of feeling. I leaned down to touch the smooth mound of a mushroom that sprouted out of nowhere after a rain shower earlier that day. I leaned down to carefully stroke the shell of a turtle that had come up from the river for who-knows-what-reason, taking care to stay out of reach of his jaws.

The wind sounded like a lost child of the universe crying at the edges of time. It was like the remaining pockets of exiled voices I read about once, weeping because they have no place of their own.

And, then, after all, I knew the sounds were those carved out of wilderness which this had been at one time. They were born of the mourning dove and the whippoorwill and, later, the wailing leftovers of passing trains. They were crafted of fires fed by the wind and left to make do for themselves in the wilderness.

They were like echoes never called out anymore, hobnobbing in vanished forests. Echoes that lost the voices they echoed. Abandoned echoes. All using the language of the river.

§§§

three
THE LAND

The sounds and smells and textures beckoned me
To sample all those riches - - they were free!

I walked farther along the river, watching the shadows of the trees mirrored in lazy waters. Even if I had been told to hurry with the cows for milking, I dawdled. I couldn't hurry past the swampy, weedy places where little fish and minnows darted here and there. A turtle poked its head out but moved back into its shell again.

After lingering there for a while, I moved on to the dropout at the curve of the river where the water swirled. Nobody knew how deep it was. We had been told that someone drowned there but it seemed unbelievable. Not in this river that I loved so much!

There could be no sweeter music that that of the river. It rippled around rocks, gurgling playfully. As it followed the long curve of its course, it hummed. As it passed over the deepest part, it boomed like the bass voices in a choir.

It pleased me to know that this was the same river Grandfather Olaf found - - the one that probably sounded mythical to Grandmother Anna at home in Sweden. This same river rose when the water was high in spring and after heavy rainfall. After which it tossed angrily upon the rocks, snarling, and growling. During long, dry spells, it became reduced to a shallow stream it seemed to drown the image of a willow tree.

After I had driven the cattle home, I still heard the music of the river.

Sometimes, standing in our yard, facing the poplar grove in the direction of the river, I stopped to listen to the rush of water - - and there it was! During spring, especially, when the peepers and the frogs filled the air with their chorus of calls, it filtered back against a background of water pounding against the bridge supports like the beat of percussive instruments.

North of our yard, a narrow wheel-rutted road ran east and west. If you followed it west, you would come to a grassy place where a store once stood. By reputation, the owners sold harness supplies, fly spray, flour and sugar, coffee and buckets of preserved herring and maybe flyswatters too.

The store provided a post office, too. Although government records do not honor its existence, the place is shown on early maps as Hedin's Post Office.

Beyond the store site, the road coming from Mora rounded a curve that would have skirted the site of Hedin's store. This was once a stagecoach trail coming out of Mora and going northward.

Before going indoors, I looked back toward the river. Walking there was easy, because I knew the knolls of the pastureland by heart. I could dodge them, walking in between, hardly looking down. It was familiar ground.

An owl hooted from a tree not far away. His lonesome sounding "hoo-hoo" was the note on which I ended my walk for the day. *Well, who?*

§§§

four

THE FIRE

Sun-baked were the forests, the pastures, fields and plains,
A tinderbox for sparks from passing trains.

Minnesota, developing from a wilderness of brush, lakes and forests, had been admitted as a state. To the south, Fort Snelling became officially established as a military post. People occupied more and more of the land, and towns sprouted up like mushrooms after rain. Railroad tracks, resembling endless metal feelers, stretched across the acres.

Drought conditions had prevailed throughout the past decade. And, increasingly, the trains proved to be hazardous as well as convenient. Sparks from the passing trains touched off fires here and there. Sometimes, those fires died out before spreading. But then, there were other times.

In 1892, the fires menaced life. The air felt heavy and danger lurked at every hand. The fires were capricious, sometimes devouring everything at hand. In other places, they burned out and left gaps before beginning again. The bent, bowed old oak tree that served as a local landmark escaped the flames. Tall, strong pine trees in the same locale left only charred heaps where they had been.

Grandfather Olaf joined the army of men who left their homes to fight the fire. Grandmother Anna and Great-Grandmother Brita Stina, left behind with the two youngest children, would have to find refuge on their own. Herman, my father, was the youngest child; his brother Edward was the other child.

Anna remembered now the storm of protest following her announcement back in Nasviken (Angsagen) Sweden, "I will not leave my mother behind!" Anna's cousin protested loudly, perhaps out of envy, "You can't drag her across the world like that! It might kill her!"

Anna's determination prevailed. Now she gave silent thanks for that decision.

They took the two small children and began walking to Mora. Anna carried Herman, my father, who was too small to walk any distance. Anna and her mother felt keenly the responsibility of these two little ones. Brita Stina, always resourceful, had brought along a leather pouch that had belonged to her father. In it, she and Anna packed wet cloths which they used for bathing their faces and those of the children.

As they labored along in the heat and smoke, a young vixen fox joined them. Her eyes were wild with fear. She must have believed that these two women with the children had some clue to safety. And then, a doe, which bleated piteously but overcame her mistrust of humans, attached herself to them. The heavy air billowing with smoke overwhelmed creatures of the wilderness and altered their animals' judgment about whom and what to trust.

Again, Brita Stina proved her value as a traveler. Water in the river became warm from the fires that burned nearby. Upon discovering that, she reached down beside a big rock. There, in that shelter, the water was cool and refreshing. She and Anna dipped their cloths into those places. They bathed their faces and those of the children. It gave them new vigor and hope.

They followed the course of the Knife River, walking in the waters of the stream. Their destination was the town of Mora. Along the way they reached the confluence of the Knife and Snake rivers. In an excitement of gushing waters, splashing and gurgling, they felt frightened at first. Soon, however, they found there was nothing to fear. The furor was only at the surface. Stalwartly, they plodded on.

The little procession reached Mora at last and before Anna's aching arms lost strength. There, they found shelter, food, and caring people. It was a godsend. Mora, named for her sister city in Sweden, offered safety as well as a few comforts, such as, a place to sleep at night, food to eat and coffee to drink. Brita Stina had picked up a turtle beside a big rock in the river. She put it into a gunny sack she had folded away with her knitting. It had been heavy to carry, but willing hands stretched out to help her when she reached destination. The gathering of refugees had turtle soup for supper. "The Turtle Lady" they called Brita Stina who laughed indulgently. She said she had been called worse things.

Olaf found his family in Mora when he returned from fighting fires to the east. He gathered them together, and they headed back to the homestead.

They found disaster waiting for them. The new house that Olaf has built was burned to the ground. The old log cabin they first inhabited, a few feet away, bore its markings of smoke, but it remained intact. The old cabin which Anna said she was finished with forever. They had outgrown it.

Now it held its charred arms open to them, and they accepted its shelter. The church, for which Olaf had set aside property, was not yet built. But, no doubt, Olaf called his forces around him. He

14

contacted whatever people he could reach, and they held a prayer service for thanksgiving.

While no written records tell us what Scripture their service was built around, but we can be sure they worshipped. The hymns they sang gave homage to the God of Love, who had brought them to the sod of this Land of the Free where they could worship in their chosen way. If quavering voices failed to carry far in the woods around them their deep feelings hovered among the wild geraniums which dared to sprout again in the wake of fires of destruction.

When they had gathered enough supplies to bake bread again, did Grandmother Anna take up her old ways? Did she still share a few loaves with the passing Indians (as they were called then)? Did she measure out some of her precious flour and sugar and salt and coffee to give to others?

Records do not report their rejoicing when they found smoked venison stored away in the root cellar which was sealed shut by a fallen tree. If wild animals had found it, they would have used it to feed their starving young.

But, amazingly, the meat was still wrapped in skins resting in a hollow and weighted with a rock.
Olaf's prayer at mealtime praised his Heavenly Father for the unexpected riches. Anna hummed an old Swedish hymn as she worked and prepared a meal.

During the late fall evenings, smoke poured from the chimney of the log cabin. Candlelight cheered the dimness inside. Olaf and Anna talked about the Old Country. And, yes, the New Country too. Their country, America.

§§§

five

THE RIVER

The waters sang and chattered as they flowed
Along where ghosts of other centuries rode.

The river was talkative. Often it seemed to me it asked bubbly, querulous questions. When the waters ran rapidly, I heard a complaining note. I'm sure it stuttered, too.

In springtime, I liked seeing its busyness. I liked watching the frothy caps of waves tossed on rocks along the way. Still, it could be forbidding at such times. I knew that if I were to stand in the midst of its action, I wouldn't be able to keep my balance.

Even the fish we saw occasionally leaping from the water were bigger and livelier than in other seasons. Once, I saw an egret fishing at the water's edge. It waited patiently until spying its prey. Then, it reached down, plucked the fish out of the water and flew away.

I felt breathless to witness such an act. I admired the skill with which the bird chose its victim and the precision with which it carried out its mission. And, still, I felt sad. There will always be victors and victims.

The greatest discovery of all was the day I stood on the bridge looking to the south and east. The steel framework of the bridge was rusty looking and I hesitated before taking hold for support.

But, suddenly, I found myself drifting, drifting. *"Why the bridge is loose from its moorings and I am going downstream with it!"* I decided. After a few seconds I could see that I had never moved at all. I had gotten a free ride while I was standing still.

I came many times after that to travel downstream again. I liked the sensation. If it was an illusion, it was one I was not ashamed to reclaim.

A boat would never have made it downstream for there were too many rocks in the riverbed. During summer months the water level was low. In some places, where the stream was quiet, lily pads formed on the surface. Sometimes I pretended a parade, and the lily pads were floats. The river was even more talkative, sometimes adding sighs of admiration.

Those moments at the river's edge were precious times. Times that I put in the keepsake part of memory so that I could call them back when ice and snow bound our lives into confining places. Then I longed for freedom, and I reached back to revisit and enjoy those scenes again.

Birds came to the river to drink. Timid little wrens stayed near stones on which they perched while drinking.

I felt defensive about the wrens whose sweet songs ran through my mind long after they stopped singing. I wanted to protect them. I rejoiced when they found places where they could light and rest or drink water.

And one day, I saw a tiny bird nest rocking like a boat. It was empty. I raged at the nest robber that had no doubt stolen the eggs and perhaps killed its inhabitants.

The river gave another dimension to my life. I liked hearing its ever-present conversation. I liked its change from a quiet, teapot-like tempest to a wildly surging, scolding stream.

Like the echoes from the bell in the church my Grandfather helped to establish that live on for me, the varied voices of the river, its moods and its constant movement, continue to be my companions.

§§§

six

THE BRIDGE

Nature challenged man's display of might,
She flung her ice chunks at the bridge both day and night.

"Turbulence," someone said, "is the force of life." I saw it, I heard it, and I felt it. There was trouble in the spring when the ice on Knife Lake broke up too suddenly. In spite of danger and possible damage to homesteads, I enjoyed the time.

Our farm property was roughly five miles south of the lake. Along that expanse of Knife River, the ice chunks galloped with awesome force, picking up speed and momentum as they traveled. From our farmhouse, I could hear them crunch and grind against each other.

Up to this point, the mighty chunks of ice met no resistance. Unleashed by the water that escaped its icy prison, they moved forward. The first stoppage they met was the iron bridge that spanned the distance from our property eastward to that of others'.

If ice piled up higher than the opening, it would pound the abutments with full force. But, if the massive, tumbling chunks of ice spilled into the swiftly moving stream, they could pass under the bridge and beyond.

The next development was anybody's guess.

In current times, people search hungrily for excitement. They look for it at tracks where autos race at breathtaking speed. They look for it in the skies, sometimes piloting frail craft among the clouds. Sadly, some look for it with an exchange of gunfire that results in loss of life.

During my childhood, I knew people who did not hunt for excitement but were part of a crisis of nature. As that crisis approached, we had phone calls from neighbors up and down the river. An undercurrent of panic ran through those calls.

People were mostly concerned with having water flood their places. I knew that our biggest worry was one that had been handed down through the years, "Will the bridge hold?"

That seemed absurd to me. The iron structure was fastened soundly to the huge beams underneath. It represented the mightiness of man's building skills. I did not know that, compared with the force of a swift current of water and tumbling ice chunks, the bridge was frail. It could crumble and be swept away.

As the days went on, fears multiplied. And as the fears multiplied farmers came to join a group huddled by the river. This was unusual for these otherwise independent farmers. The American spirit burned in their veins. "We don't need help. We get along by ourselves!"

One of them had watched lightning strike his barn, causing it to burn down. Others had seen grasshoppers devour a promising field of oats. But all of them, as a unit, were scared by the force of the river with its ice floes tossed like playthings on the rapidly moving water.

A neighborhood spirit had awakened. Now, the men gathered wood and started bonfires. One of them brought an old enamel coffee pot. The others brought cups from home and a supply of lump sugar.

They drank coffee and waited in shifts, controlled by "chore-time." They took turns watching, afraid to see what they were watching for. They drank coffee and told tales. They spat tobacco juice and sounded more jovial than they felt.

When the days turned colder for a spell, they relaxed and breathed more easily. For a while the thawing process was held at bay. When it began again, maybe it would be at a slower rate, making for an easier break-up.

A child of twelve years, I stood with our Papa and watched too, enjoying the novelty of the bonfire. Enjoying the strangeness of the neighborhood spirit that was not always there.

Enjoying the conversation of the men who seldom met together, kept apart by the mix of Norwegians and Swedes who hung onto grudges left over from the Old Country.

Usually, I did not stay by the river too long. I went home where it was warmer. I could go upstairs to the windows in the landing. Those were windows offering a vista. I could see the rolling terrain of the big field to the south. I could see the home of my maternal grandparents, Nub and Julia Wigen, in the distance. I could see the spiny winter profiles of trees that ran through our pastureland all the way to the bridge, now in danger.

From a vantage point, I could see the bonfires too. Sometimes the flames leaped high. At other times the fire burned low and only a thin wisp of smoke rose into the air. I dubbed in the rest from memory.

At night, if the wind was in the east, the pounding and hissing of the ice monsters crept inside the house. It was hard to sleep knowing about all that activity so close at hand.

Through the years I grew up, while the river offered its periodic drama, the bridge held fast to its moorings.

Later, a dam built on Knife Lake changed our lives. Except for one instance when flooding water broke the dam, there was never again a threat to the bridge whose rusted girders looked so strong to me.

When I grew older, I remembered that our Papa had said he was sure glad that was over. I hardly believed him. I believed, instead, that he too had been lifted out of the daily humdrum of tending animals. Seeing drama like that which the river furnished, first-hand, seldom happens to ordinary people.

The bridge stood for many years before it was replaced by a newer, modern structure. The old bridge disappeared with the passing of an era. Like the pioneers themselves, the bridge had been triumphant over nature's brutal forces.

§§§

seven

THE COOPERATIVE

When the pasture-grass stood tall and rich and green,
The milk we sold was richer than we'd ever seen.

I remember them yet! Usually, three or four milk cans stood beside the driveway. They looked like tin soldiers in parade formation, their lids resembling crowned hats pulled snugly over their ears. While I cannot say how much milk they held, I would guess ten to fifteen gallons.

They occupied a space under the protective branches of a big oak tree. On summer days the shade helped keep them cool. When the driver came late, they stood through early afternoon hours seeming to hug their shadows around them.

During winter months, we traded the anxiety of the milk staying cool and sweet for that of hoping it would not freeze. Whatever the case, the cans looked lonely and vulnerable out there waiting for the driver to arrive. We looked out the kitchen window frequently, as if our concern would somehow keep them safer.

The milk that came from our cattle was on its way. After the truck picked up the cans, they would be joined by others destined for the Co-Op in Mora. Each container bore the identity of the farm from which it came. Each would be tested and the amount of butterfat recorded, as well as cleanliness and general appearance. The experienced eyes of the inspectors did not miss much.

The place that housed the Co-Op was a building with odd angles; no doubt because several additions had taken place since the original building went up. The mill distributed a thin layer of white residue over everything on the premises. I wrote my name in big letters on the floor. Sacks of ground grain sagged against each other along the wall. They looked like small children huddled together, waiting to be let inside.

Part of the building, separated by bins, housed whole grain - - some for feed, some for seed. The place was messy looking with piles of grain left here and there. Shovels lay helter-skelter on the floor.

My father's neat granary put the place to shame.

Milk from our farm, deposited in this place, was pasteurized and sold to customers. At regular intervals, checks arrived in the mail.

My father examined them suspiciously and occasionally grumbled "They get smaller every time!"

But, checks for the milk were not our only payment. The Co-Op was an organization farmers in Minnesota joined so they could buy and sell products as a group. We were members of this organization. At regular intervals, the Co-Op elected officers and a board of directors. They were the governing body.

And, at regular intervals, a shareholder's check arrived in our mail. It, too, was carefully slid into the cupboard alongside Papa's moustache cup which I had never seen him use. There, it was hidden except for the crisp end of the envelope which protruded.

I used to peer at it, occasionally, knowing, that check represented some relief from the threat of poverty.

When Papa went into town, he removed the check and slipped it into the pocket of his jacket. That check was the only cash payment we received on a regular basis from the sale of our product which was milk. It was the token of our worthwhileness. It stood for some provision of buying power.

Our eggs provided a ready source of income, although it was too small to cover everything. Supposedly, they were Mama's hens, and Mama's eggs. In a household where cash was so scarce, however, the egg money covered a broad area. It bought Papa the occasional cigar or snuff. It bought ice cream for anyone fortunate enough to be in town at the same time the eggs were sold.

While the eggs were picked and cleaned on a daily basis, I was often sent to the henhouse to round up another half dozen eggs to fill the crate. This chore involved some risk, for the hens did not approve of being interrupted at work. Their pecks on my flesh involved no danger, but they were a nuisance. I carried grudges against the offenders.

The egg money might purchase a coat or jacket or buy medicinal products. Ironically, it bought the feed for the chickens that produced the eggs. Sometimes, it was saved up to buy baby chicks in the springtime so that more chickens could produce more eggs.

Cleaned and packed into crates the eggs saved the day more than once. We pilfered as many as we could for use in the kitchen. Fried eggs made a meal if we had no meat.

At times, when egg production was high, the kitchen turned out large amounts of sponge and angel food cake. We could even count on floating islands for dessert, (recipe included) at least on Sundays. What a treat to anticipate.

I tried to manage my chores when that happened so I could sneak in at intervals to watch the floating islands in the oven. At first the concoction was just a creamy mixture in the process of baking.

If I timed my oven-checks to see the first blobs of egg whites baking to a gentle brown, my excitement mounted. "Don't slam the oven door!" My older sisters warned.

I didn't, for I knew the risk of ruining the floating islands. At that point I could taste those brown puffed islands that would be portioned out to everyone at the table. It made the water pails I carried seem lighter. It made the chore of feeding calves a little less of a drudgery.

Even as a small child, I recognized the appearances of prosperity. When the pastures were lush, the cattle produced accordingly. If I looked toward the driveway and saw *five* milk cans I felt a thrill of security. Now, that check my father slipped between two cups in the glassed-in cabinet would be bigger.

Conversely, when the pasture was brown for lack of rain, I felt worried. Only two cans of milk to deliver to the Co-Op? Fear loitered just below the surface.

That big building called the Co-Op furnished another community benefit. A little door off the street opened into a lounge area for the benefit of the country women. If you felt ill, you could lie down on a sofa provided.

There was a table and a few chairs, too. If you were going to be in town for some time you could bring a sandwich and eat it there. A few of the chairs were straight. You could pull them up to the table. Others were of the lounging variety where you could rest for a few minutes. While the furnishings were not luxurious, they offered all we knew of benefits granted by the outside world.

Wives of merchants and professional men maintained the lounge for the Co-Op members and their families. They contributed such simple articles as a pillow and a blanket. It was all part of the benefits of the Co-Op.

Co-Ops meant people pooling their resources to get the greatest benefits. While the shareholder's check arriving in the mail at regular intervals was tangible evidence of being a part of it, the simple lounge offered proof of our connection with The Cooperative.

Members of our extended family held jobs in that mystical-sounding place "The Cities." They talked about job benefits. Our benefits came from a loosely-knit organization called The Cooperative.

We took pride in its giving us a role in the commercial world.

RECIPE FOR FLOATING ISLANDS

2	Cups of milk	5	Egg yolks
½	Teaspoon salt		Sugar
¼	Teaspoon vanilla extract		
1	Egg white (at room temperature)		Water

Combine egg yolks, milk, salt with 2/3 cup sugar. Cook in a double boiler, stirring constantly. If mixture coats the spoon it is done (about 15 minutes). Add vanilla extract and stir.

Meanwhile beat the egg white in a small bowl. When small peaks form, you have beaten them well enough.

Gradually sprinkle two tablespoons of sugar over the egg whites. Beat that until the sugar has dissolved completely.

Then, the custard should be spooned into dessert dishes. When the egg whites have been formed, remove them with a slotted spoon, place them into the oven and brown them. Watch them carefully so that the meringue top is only gently browned. When they are browned, put one blob on top of each of the dishes with the custard mixture. You have made floating islands.

§§§

eight

THE COOMPA

Some would say our meal was "peasants fare,"
But our concern was that we got our share.

"Oh, boy!" we said unanimously, upon learning that our supper dish was "klub," a Scandinavian concoction. Klub was a favorite*

Actually, we could see what was going on in the preparations already under way. A grinder stood mounted on the edge of the kitchen table. Newspapers spread below caught the drippings as potatoes crunched through the metal spirals of the gadget.

Stove tenders attempted to get the kitchen stove up to tropical-like temperatures. On the kitchen table laid a slab of salt pork, just extracted from the layers preserved in a big crock. Although salt pork became tiresome to us during winter months - - after the fresh meat was gone - - it acquired new appeal in klub.

Some of the work for this adventure in eating was a joint effort. I usually won the task of carrying in more wood so we could stoke up the stove to top level performance for several hours.

Others in the family turned the handle of the grinder, changed the paper set there to catch the drippings, supplied flour to Mama and cut salt pork into chunks. Although Mama was in charge, making klub was a community effort. As the potatoes were being ground, Mama dumped them into a huge mixing bowl. There, she added flour to the potato mixture. She used no measuring devices. If you asked her how much flour she put in she would say, "some". If you asked how much salt to add, she said, "a pinch or two." (That caused me to look in bewilderment at the difference between her pinch and mine.) She added a few pieces of salt pork and began gathering the mixture into balls.

These balls called "klub" (or coompa) were roughly three inches in diameter. After Mama had finished that operation, she placed the balls into a huge kettle, covered them with water, and the cooking process began. Cooking time depended on the amount of klub in the kettle. It required attention from the cook and good judgment as well.

The kettle we used was probably twenty inches in diameter and eighteen inches high. Getting the water to a simmering point required considerable time. Then, the cooks must make allowance for cooking through the bulk of the potato balls.

Although klub was safe in out heavy kettle, I stirred it, nevertheless, with Mama's big wooden spoon. It would be a shame if the klub would stick to the bottom and scorch. Then, too, we must be sure that all the potato balls had the advantage of being in hot places in the kettle (such as, next to the kettle walls) and that all were immersed in bubbling water.

When the barn chores were finished, we drew up to the table for a sumptuous meal of klub served with butter. Our own wonderful butter fresh from the last churning. Golden as the sun, and brimming with good taste.

After the meal, we put the remaining portions of klub into the big kettle from which the water had been drained. Even in the cooling process, they must be kept separate so they wouldn't stick to each other.

The secret of success, of course, was in the preparation. As with all food, that which is put together indifferently is eaten with indifference.

That is equally true of food for the spirit. The spirit must be fed - - in fact, has been known to die if not fed.

Little conversation accompanied this repast which our Scandinavian family relished. We hardly noticed, for we ate heartily of the tasty and satisfying meal. Out attention was being consumed as well as the food itself.

The food, made of potatoes, was heavy. Papa tried to tell a couple of his hired man jokes, but they fell to their death in the center of the table. The disappointment was too much for Papa who then lapsed into silence, occupied with digesting the klub.

When we had eaten our fill for the first meal, the rest was put away carefully. We would come to the re-heated klub tomorrow as enthusiastically as we had done today.

The klub would cool enough overnight. During the cooling process, the potato balls were kept away from each other so they wouldn't stick together. Then, we sliced the klub balls into one-half inch slices.

These were fried in butter until they were crisp and well-browned. If klub was welcomed the first time, it was certainly hailed as a treat the second time.

The lowly potato had been exalted!

One klub contained enough salt pork to offer protein for our meal. That satisfied dietary requirements.

The simple meal, given attention, elevated the lowly potato to desirable heights. "Klub for supper?" "Yes - - and hooray!"

*Also, sometimes called "coompa".

<u>Klub Potato Dumplings</u>
4 Cups Grated Raw Potatoes   2 Cups Flour
1 Tablespoon Salt   ½ lb. Fresh or Salt
Pork

Mix all the ingredients, except the pork. Shape into balls with your hands. Put small pieces of pork in center of dumpling. Add enough flour to keep from sticking. Drop dumplings into boiling water. Cover and boil one hour. Stir occasionally, to prevent dumplings from sticking to the bottom of kettle. Also, watch or the water will boil over the side of the vessel.

Serve hot with butter and also dip fork size pieces into cream. The pork is to give it flavor. If you cook them in broth, you will not need the pork. Serve with crisp fried side pork.

This recipe is taken from "The Wigen Family Heritage Cookbook." Recipe was from Gertrude Norberg's cousin's wife, Valborg Benson.

§§§

nine

THE PRESSED MEAT

With care we took the cover off and looked,
Into the boiler where the hog's head cooked.

The project had been brewing for days. I had seen a passing glimpse of the hog's head left by itself in the granary, and I knew the day had come for the preparation of the syllta or head cheese.

If it had been possible to get past the grisly business of cutting up a whole hog's head, we would have. We had to be determined for the task ahead. If Mama found it revolting to have the eye of a dead pig fixed on her as she moved about the kitchen, she did not let on.

Too steady a diet of salt pork, with occasional meals of ground beef patties or canned meat, readied us for something to vary our meals. The prospect of syllta was a welcome one.

Surprisingly, there is a lot of good meat on the head of a hog. Getting rid of the eyes is necessary before you can begin to anticipate something better.

The meat cutting went on, requiring sharp knives and steady hands. Gradually, the meat piled up and the bones became a pile, scarcely resembling the pig that had squealed loudly from its pen, a few hours before.

Even though I had no fondness for hogs (on the hoof, or any other way, I felt some sadness the day I knew our biggest hog would be sacrificed for our sakes). I had found his squealing most annoying when I put food in his trough. He was smelly, and he pushed at me when I reached through the fence, but I could not justify those grievances as being enough to cost his life.

The day of the butchering, Papa got help from someone in the neighborhood for the actual slaughter. While Papa did not complain, I noticed a white line around his mouth. Marking that, I knew it was not easy for Papa to kill any creature.

The time had arrived, however, and we were steeled against the loss of an animal from our premises. I found a remote place on the second floor of our farmhouse, and I hid away there, refusing to pay attention until I knew the hog was no longer alive.

Then, Papa and the neighbor took care of the grisly matter. Once the animal was fastened on a huge hook from the granary ceiling, I felt safe from the trauma. The butchering process went on through the day, with chops being pared off for frying, roasts being set aside, ribs for special preparation, and meat kept separate and set away to cure in salt.

The latter was done with crocks which we kept in the cellar. Our parents' long experience had taught them how much salt to add with the meat to cure it. After the meat had been salted away, we covered the big crocks with a couple of layers of flour sacks and tied strings around them to keep them airtight.

Only Mama or Papa untied those strings and removed pieces of salt pork for our meals. The slabs of pork probably weighed five pounds each. If the hog had been fed properly, the slabs of pork were laced with strips of meat. The rest fried away into fat.

I was impressed with the fact that our Mama, along with all the other skills she had acquired, must know how to cure meat.

While we grew very tired of eating salt pork, as the winter went on, we relished the strips of pork fried on top of the stove after butchering. When it was fried right, the fat grew crisp, and the meat fried until it cooked through. When the skin was browned to doneness, it became crisp and tasty.

By the time the pork chops reached our table for supper that evening, we had all been involved with the butchering process. My job may have been to cart away bones and refuse removed from the pieces separated for canning, or salting or grinding for sausage.

In one of the outbuildings, we had begun a pile of bones and cuttings considered unfit for human consumption. We kept refuse of this kind away from the dog and the chickens. Whatever tidbits found their way into the chicken troughs or into the dog dish were carefully superintended.

Papa hauled the rest away. He dug a huge hole in the ground where he disposed of the refuse. At times, packs of dogs congregated in the neighborhood. They always looked for refuse which, if found, they fought over. A farmer had to be responsible about removal of such matter that could cause problems. Dogs fighting over grisly treasures might be ugly and dangerous to have around.

Little by little, all the precious meat was preserved or stored in some fashion. Nothing went to waste. Our mouths watered when we thought of the chops that would grace our dinner table that evening. If Mama and Papa felt troubled over eating this animal that had been a part of our farm menagerie, they said nothing.   It seems strange, now, that we were hardened to sacrificing an animal.

A platter of fresh pork chops on the supper table was a treat that words could hardly express. Juicy and brown, they gave us a dinner too delicious for mere words.

Our first meal of sliced syltta made from meat cut off the pig's head became a kind of banquet. There was no question of whether or not we liked it. It was tender, fresh meat rather than cured. It was well-prepared and satisfying. It was a treat.

Since we were products of the farm life that required sacrifice of animals for our meat, we did not ask a lot of questions. We enjoyed the good food served to us. Fond feelings for creatures inhabiting our lives were considered too much of a luxury to hang onto for long.

One instance of indulging in sentiment stays in my mind. We had raised a few sheep, mostly as an indulgence to Papa who considered them to be harmless, and "nice to have around.   One day Papa announced that it was time we had some mutton. He would butcher a sheep. He got up in a purposeful way and went outside to carry out his plan..

Sometime afterward, he came back and sat heavily on a kitchen chair...

His hands trembled out of control.

Papa pushed his hat backon his head. In a shaky voice he said, "I couldn't do it. I just couldn't do it."

So, the sheep continued to roam our yard, safe from any molestation. They were not sources of mutton to us. They were just sheep, too defenseless to be sacrificed for our appetites and nice to have around.

Recipe for Head Cheese (Pressylta)

3 to 5 lbs. Fresh Side Pork* or 1 pig's head.
3 lbs. breast or shoulder of veal
5 or 6 Bay Leaves
Allspice to taste.
2 Tablespoons salt
10 Whole White Peppers

Soak pig's head overnight in water in a laundry tub and boil two hours on top of stove. Skim off sediment. Add other ingredients and let simmer until meat is soft. Strain and save liquid.

Wring out a towel in water and place inside of round mold. Remove skin from pork and place half in bottom of dish, on top of towel. Then alternate with slices of pork and veal. Season well with each layer. Top with remainder of pork skin.

Gather together and tie securely. Place in heated liquid and boil for fifteen minutes. Let stand in heavy press overnight. Will keep in brine for one to two weeks.

(If desired, various vegetables may be added while boiling, which greatly improves the flavor.)

*Fresh Side Pork *can be purchased at a meat market*

§§§

ten

THE RUMMEGROT

Some thought this was the richest kind of fare,
The choicest (if you liked it) anywhere.

But, I don't like rummegrot," I complained. Even worse, I could feel the heaving objection of my digestive system. It revolted if anything thick slid down my throat. "You'll like it when you start eating it," Mama said, unsympathetically.

She was wrong I not only did not like rummegrot, I hated it! Soon after eating a couple of mouthfuls, I headed for the back door. Outside, safely beyond the back steps, I tossed away all evidence of the Scandinavian so-called delicacy.

I did not even like to watch members of my family eating rummegrot. They ate it from plates where the porridge lay in quivering dollops. The latter had been topped by amber blobs of melted butter, skimmed from cream while it cooked.

I had been watching with some revulsion since Mama took out the heavy kettle. Into this kettle, she poured cream skimmed off the top of one day's milk cans. The cream had heated slowly on the stove.

When I tended the stove during this period of time, I learned that the fire must burn steadily, but not too hot. Even in a big kettle like the one Mama used, cream could scorch. While I did not like this Scandinavian delicacy, neither did I want to be responsible for spoiling it.

Mama made rummegrot skillfully. While cream heated on the stove, she stirred in flour, and then, kept skimming off the butter that rose to the top. That was proof of the high butterfat content of the milk in which Papa exhibited such chest-thumping pride.

The only comfort for being an outsider of rummegrot admirers was to consort with the wood elves that lurked around the woodpile until it was safe for me to go in by the stove.

As usual, Mama did justice to the recipe that - - as with so may others - - she carried around in her head. "Rummegrot?" well, that was filed right over here under "Treasures from the Old Country." A woman like Mama never misfiled anything as important as that.

Mama was a picture worth remembering as she prepared her rummegrot. Her cheeks got rosier from heat of the stove. Her footsteps had a confident lilt. She was sure of herself - - in command of the enterprise. She looked happy as she hummed hymns like, "O Master, let me walk with thee."

Even though I did not care for the Norwegian porridge-like concoction, I found its preparation interesting.

"Is this the way Grandmother Julia made rummegrot?" I asked.

"M-h'm."

"Who taught her how to make it?"

"Grandma Olausen."

"Is she the lady who thought God was Norwegian?"

"M-h'm."

While she stood stirring the rummegrot, Mama filled in bits of our family history. I learned that

Grandfather Nub was a singer with more than the usual talent, and Grandmother Julia an expert in the art of knitting.

Caught up as I was in the preparation of rummegrot, I became reconciled to that dish, even though it did not agree with me. It was a traditional food served in celebration of the harvest season.

<u>Recipe for Rummegrot</u>
One pint Cream.
1/6 Cup Cream of Wheat
1+ Tsp. Salt
1+ Tbsp. Sugar

3+ Cups Milk
½+ Cups Flour
Cinnamon

Boil the cream for at least ten minutes.

Add 1/6 cup of cream of wheat and cook for five minutes. Then the butter should come out. Pour off the butter.

Add 1 Teaspoon salt and 1 Tablespoon sugar to about three cups of milk and ½ cup flour. Cook until fairly thick. Not too thick.

More milk, and proportionate amounts of salt and sugar may be added to the first mixture, if more is needed.

Dish out on plates. Sprinkle with sugar and cinnamon if desired. Put the butter on top. I used nine cups of milk, but should have made more. Maybe four times recipe, maybe three cups flour and twelve cups milk. If so, boil that part for 30 minutes.

§§§

eleven

THE FEVER

Our neighbors and our kinfolk stayed away,
The risk of 'catching it' too high a price to pay.

Each of the hammer blows that pounded nails into a sign on the door by order of the Kanabec County Public Health Association; "Quarantined," it read in big black letters. We had scarlet fever.

This sign warned people away until they lifted the ban. We were like a shifting island in a sea of uncertainty.

I, the victim, was probably better off than the others, for I lay too sick to care about anything. Days and nights merged into one another. Denied the normal routine of mealtimes, going to bed and getting up, I became a prisoner to the unnatural state of a sick person.

My recollections are patchy and unrelated. The memories I piece together seem not to belong to each other. It is like viewing a pageant from afar and having the characters change positions while you watch.

I coughed, terrible coughing that seemed to rip my insides out. The home recipe for relieving such coughs, a simple and dreadful medicine, reads as follows: One tablespoon of kerosene with hot milk. That was guaranteed to upset your stomach. Even if it stopped the coughing, it upset the whole system to such a degree that coughing seemed relatively unimportant.

My throat was sore.   Our home recipe for treating that was to rub generous amounts of a preparation called musterole on the chest and back. This treatment resulted in a burning sensation that eclipsed all other discomfort.

I entered into an invalid's life - - a lonely life, unpeopled and desolate. It had no boundaries. It did not include structured meal hours. It held forth a bleak sameness that stretched from sunup until the weak winter sun drained away into the western horizon.   I knew the range of farm activities; the sounds of milk pails with handles clanging against the sides like castanets. I could hear milk being poured from one vessel to another. The gushing of milk that filled a pitcher, put away for home use. The next step consisted of straining the milk and setting it to cool until pouring it into the milk cans for shipping to the Co-Op.

And, I knew the smell of fresh milk, a heavy cloying smell at once pleasant and overwhelming.

The smell of baking bread was the best of all. Even if I had no appetite for it after it was baked, I rode the waves of anticipation. As it wafted through the rooms, I felt overjoyed to have a part in this everyday, homey part of life in our farmhouse.

I knew the sounds of meal making.   Fat splattering in a pan on the stove. Pieces of meat browning in a busy pattern of activity, with an accompanying smell of meat in the process of cooking. It sounded good to me until I tried to eat it and then found myself with no appetite.

One neighbor, Pete S., a rather brash and over-talkative kind of man, came to visit in the kitchen just beyond my sick room. It was brave of him to come. He and Papa did not always get along well, and yet, here he was offering any kind of help possible.

When he was present, the door to my room was closed. Some of the conversation that took place was not for my ears. I heard them say "Tom J's boy is very low." Even without more explanation I knew they were saying Tom J's boy had scarlet fever, too. When Pete S. returned one day, it was to report that Tom J's boy was dead.

Great fears swept over me then, for I was certain that would be my destiny. "How is she doing?" I heard Pete S. ask. Muffled voices kept me from catching all the words but the inference was clear. *I wasn't doing very well.*

Pete S. was an obliging man. He took our eggs to town, had them graded, and brought home the money. He went to the grocery store and picked up the items Mama needed most.

He drank coffee with Mama and Papa, too, his company welcome in our house from which other visitors had been banned by the quarantine.

His presence did not satisfy my sisters though. They felt agitated by the restrictions of the quarantine set to cover a period of two weeks' time. That might not seem long, but they felt cut off from their friends. Our household came through the duration in a sort of a capsule of loneliness.

For a long time, Mama would not even let my sisters play the organ and sing hymns. Those activities were considered too noisy to be tolerated with a sick person in the household.

My funny, fever-stricken world rocked in a topsy-turvy way through the night hours. The fever was highest then, and I got out of bed to roam through the house. Papa, afraid I would go outside, followed me until I was back in bed again.

During those fever-raided hours, I had strange dreams. A recurring one was about someone I dubbed Mrs. Andy Gump (comic strip character). She wandered through my dreams every night holding high in front of her, a shiny bright red purse. I wanted that purse. My night hours were spent in dream-clad pursuit of the woman, always with that little red purse held high in front of her.

I stayed right behind her until someone put me back to bed.

Eventually, the illness wore down, its severity losing its grip, day by day. We were all worn out. Mama and papa from anxiety and from their nursing concerns. I, ravaged by the fevers, the coughing, and the suspension of all normal activity. My oldest sister helped me pass the time by reading to me. Those periods were bright oases in a desert of endless hours.

Finally, a man from the health association came out to take down the quarantine sign. My sisters rejoiced for they could go back to school.

A mark of my progress was that I was removed from the couch in the dining room to be placed on Mama and Papa's bed in their bedroom during daytime hours. While that change seemed exciting, the bedroom was some distance from the kitchen where a great deal of the family activity took place.

By this time, I had lost my voice. Nothing remained but a hoarse kind of whisper. I had no way of communicating with other parts of the house. "Here" Mama suggested. "Rap on the side of the dresser."

The suggestion was well-intentioned but fraught with frustration. While the rest of the household resumed normal activity, I was marooned in my new quarters.

Desperate for a drink of water, one day, I ventured out to the kitchen and was scolded soundly. "Why didn't you rap?" Mama fussed. I showed her my reddened knuckles, where the skin was irritated from repeated rapping on the dresser.

Recovery came on slow, plodding feet, and I missed a few weeks of school. Now I could trade on my record of good marks, my ability to come bounding back.

But, it was not that easy. Severe illnesses often leave side effects. In addition to the harsh cough that persisted, I suffered attack after attack of pleurisy. Because that illness had a technical sounding name, it was something the neighbors could pick up and work over. I heard them in the kitchen when they came to visit. "Why, land sakes," one of them said, "one thing lead to another until the poor soul died!"

Not much comfort when you were struggling to feel well enough to resume normal activity and make up for lost school hours.

When I returned to school, one of my schoolmates said to me "We heard you were gonna die, but you didn't after all".

I thought she seemed disappointed.

I suffered a kind of mental relapse, having to deal with the anxiety all over again.

Yet, the general tenor of the household had improved. Papa could resume his trips to town. Neighbors and relatives could stop in for coffee. My sisters could bring home friends to take up to their bedrooms for sessions of chatter and gossip.

Pete S. stopped in often. I didn't even mind when he gave me the usual "Hello there, powder face, how ya feelin'?" I remembered he had been our Good Samaritan during our days of the quarantine.

When I finally got back to school, I had mixed feelings about being well enough to do that.

For one thing, I traded the anxiety over my illness for one less crucial but troubling, nevertheless. *Would I be able to pass the test given on fractions that loomed before me?* The teacher, out of kindness, spent some time with me studying before the test so that I passed.

An additional concern was whether or not I would advance to the next grade in the coming year after missing those weeks of school.

My appetite was poor and bringing a cold lunch to school did nothing to appeal to it. Mama even put in a hard-boiled egg. I felt touched by that, because I heard her say the egg count had fallen far below the

Not wanting to hurt her feelings, I stopped on my way home, and dumped out the things I could not eat. There was no conversation with the elves or other little people. Just a grim resolution to dispose of the leftover food scraps before anyone saw them. When I had walked a ways and looked back, I noted the crows were disposing of the food. *Now Mama would never know!*

My energy came back bit by bit. It was so gradual that I hardly noticed. It was not until I got an "A" in geography that I begun to take an interest in studying again.

One day, before I left school, the teacher asked, "Would you like to read this?" I stared in surprise. It was a shiny copy of *Rebecca of Sunnybrook Farm.*

"How did we get the book?" I asked, breathlessly.

46

"Esther Boyd, the Superintendent of Schools brought it out here for us," Juanita Myers, the teacher, replied.

I turned it over in my hands, loving the feel of its cover. I turned the leaves, awed by the shiny paper and sharp print.

"Oh, thank you." I said. "I'll be careful with it."

My convalescence had really begun now. I had a book to read. I felt sure I could lose myself in this one. It may have been the first new book I had ever had in my hands! I could hardly wait to begin reading.

§§§

twelve
THE MORTGAGE

We lived in haunted houses, you might say,
The ghost foreclosure lurked along the way.

On a small farm such as ours in Knife Lake Township, Kanabec County Minnesota, our means of livelihood stood in full view. We had watched the crops from their first pale green shoots in the spring until they matured.

In the background, other activities took place. A garden must be planted and attended. We must take off the storm windows and put on screens. When baby chicks came along they must be fed, watered and protected from predators. Yet, the fields of grain in the forefront commanded our attention. They reminded us daily of their importance to our welfare. They supplied the feed to chickens and livestock.

Times were hard. The local banker held our mortgage. That was common practice. We knew he could "call it in" any time he wanted to. In such an instance, we would have to come up with the money to pay off the mortgage or lose our farm.

Reminders of that precarious state left us feeling shaky. I thought of that every time Grandmother Julia and Grandfather Nub (maternal grandparents) came to visit us. Grandfather Nub "joked" a lot. He often came into the house saying "Mama and I are going to the Poor Farm now." I felt the knot in my stomach swelling until it almost crowded out my breath.

Grandmother quickly said "Papa's joking." But, joking aside, the Poor Farm - - or living in housing provided by some kind of charity - - became the fate of many farmers like ourselves. We lived at the mercy of a banker or his designated agent. Even if you did your best to get along with him, you were in danger of his picking your farm for foreclosure.

During the drought of the 1930's that fear crept closer. If there were no crops a farmer could not even pay off the interest on his loan. The sum of money we owed took on an almost visible shape and form.

So, it was into suspicion and fear that Franklin Delano Roosevelt, as President of the United States, presented his plans to save the Americans from an awful fate. Miners, steelworkers, auto workers, and railroad workers, as well as farmers, fell under his promise of sweeping reforms.

It is no wonder that President Roosevelt's Fireside Chats had such popular appeal. On the specified nights, we sat - - grouped together - - in the dining room of our farmhouse where we had never gathered before except for meals. There, with a squeaky, squawky, radio reception that sometimes faded out altogether we compressed our anxieties and offered them to the President of the United States.

Then-President Roosevelt had a mellow voice. It kept us spellbound as we listened. His words were plain and unmistakable. He promised "a chicken in every pot."

We became launched into an untried set of events that certainly could not remove all worries, but at least, relieved an overwhelming pressure of concerns, both distant and immediate.

At first we doubted President Roosevelt. He was too smooth. He might intend to improve living conditions for other people, but, surely, not us. Yet, we listened. No one had ever talked to ordinary people in this manner. Never before, had there been a radio to transmit such a message. The time was right.

He touched, briefly, on the way he would manage such programs as those that promised help. And, out of our disbelief, we searched hungrily for something in the Minneapolis Journal to give weight to his spoken words. To our surprise, we found such evidence. It took place under headings like "the farm relief" bill, the Home Owners Loan Corporation, and, yes, even the WPA. The latter we renamed, We Poke Along, based on our witnessing some men on WPA road crews who leaned on their shovel handles.

The fact that something happened to bear out the President's promises reassured us. Such promises would help finance farm operations, taking them from the hands of the banker who might be tempted to play out grudges.

Strange that it should be the radio, seemingly a device for entertainment, that brought hope into our lives. A simple boxy looking gadget, with two or three small knobs for tuning, sometimes it squealed unmercifully with the static transmitted, almost drowning out the words being broadcast. It's amazing that the radio had power to offer reassurance to scores of lower income people.

There would, of course, still be uncertainties. Farmers found they could plan again, despite an awareness that not all of our problems had been solved. For the notion that someone cared, even someone as far away as Washington D.C., seemed like a scene from a fairytale.

The public, at that time, was carefully shielded from the fact that Franklin Delano Roosevelt was crippled by polio. At my age, I did not question the fact that photos showed him sitting down. We knew nothing of his gallant efforts to stand and walk again, all of them in vain. Details of his illness were hidden. He stood in front of the cameras with his braces locked in place to hide his disability.

The Father of The New Deal must not be less than perfect - - in appearance, at least.

The New Deal could not protect us from the hazards of living. It could and did give us a mooring that was better than anything we had known.

§§§

thirteen

THE THRESHERS

I missed the whispers of the stalks of grain,
That caught the language of the wind and rain.

Preparation of the soil for spring planting consumed countless hours of a farmer's time. The plowing, harrowing and fertilizing were virtually hidden operations. Each required planning as well as labor.

Sometimes I saw little of Papa except glimpses of him in a cloud of dust. He came into the house for lunch, ate hurriedly, and then disappeared again until later in the day. I brought coffee to him in the morning, and in the afternoon. He barely stopped for those periods before he was on the way again.

Being responsible for trivial jobs gave me a personal investment in the crops as they appeared and grew.

By the time the crops became visible, we were aware of the unshielded nature of those plants. Late one afternoon, Papa had a cup of coffee and then set out on foot through the oat field east of the house on a tour of inspection. I noticed that he stopped at intervals to run his hands through the stalks of grain.

Sometimes he flushed out pheasants gorging themselves on the riches they found. They need not fear Papa, for he was not a hunter. At other times, he might come upon a rabbit that bounded out and away after his privacy had been invaded. Gophers darted here and there, and overhead, hawks followed their antics with interest.

What Papa had to say when he returned from the field was of vital interest to us. Maybe he would not speak until supper time. The amount of food he put on his plate drew my attention. With relief, I noted that he helped himself to another scoop of mashed potatoes and filled the cavity with gravy.

I relaxed a little then. At last, he spoke, "A little wild mustard mixed in with the oats," he said "but nothing to speak of. Hardly any thistle."

With mutual relief, the rest of us sighed, and I took another helping of potatoes, too. We could live with wild mustard so long as it did not take over the oat field, or the barley field as the case might be. And thistle, if allowed to take over, could spoil a crop.

That concern was behind us now. But, as the days passed and the grain grew higher, we watched every storm cloud with suspenseful concern. We examined it from the time it appeared. Often, the dark blue clouds with frothy edges produced wind. We saw how they advanced toward us and waited to judge their intensity.

My stomach lurched when I saw a cloud approaching. It seemed as though I controlled its development by the amount of worry it caused me. Even at twelve years of age, I noted all the particulars about threatening weather for it controlled our welfare. When the outer edges of clouds sported zigzags of lightning, I stopped whatever I was doing and gave the sky my full attention. If, by chance, the clouds separated and blow away, I felt the anxiety lift.

Another possible source of trouble was the increase in the grasshopper population. Once before, we had watched helplessly as grasshoppers stripped the oat field of its grain. They left bare stalks that bent in the wind and seemed to weep the loss. Anxiety ripped through the neighborhood as farmers assessed the damage and wondered how to start over.

At last, the season had drawn to its peak. The tempo of our rural life picked up, for now it included other people. The grain was cut, and the threshers would come to our farm. Papa contacted the local farmers to come on the appointed day. Mama and her crew of children made ready for the task of feeding everyone.

All of the hard work of the year paled to nothing compared to the work of feeding that hard-working bunch of men. We must gather vegetables for the big meal to be prepared. And, Mama selected the chickens that would be sacrificed for the meal. She would choose carefully, making sure the good "layers" were not picked by mistake. You could not say where her attentions were needed most.

When the day dawned, we got up early to fling our energies into the day's requirements. One of us swept the floors, dusted rugs, and even stopped to whisper encouragement to the houseplants. Someone else carried water to replenish the stove reservoir and teakettle. And, still another person answered the telephone. Mostly phone calls from neighbor women who called to ask if the threshers were really at our place. They wanted to give weight to their gossip.

The big thresher entered our yard with its furor of steam and noise. Teams of horses went into the fields and brought back the bundles of grain Papa had cut to be fed into the maws of the threshing machine.

The rig arrived at about 9:00 a.m. By 10:30 it was time to bring coffee and sandwiches, and cake to the men. They ate and drank with gusto, stopping to praise Mama's excellent bread and cake. Proper manners required that of them, but when empty plates returned to the kitchen, they said even more.

No other event throughout the year warranted so much housecleaning as having the threshers. We had inspected every corner. One wall along the dining room that was notorious for collecting dust curls received the strictest scrutiny. We even polished the keys of the organ although no one would venture into the living room.

At noon, the threshers came into the house for their big meal. We placed a wash bowl on a stool outside the door. Some of the men washed themselves before eating. Others did not bother. The dirt and debris they carried in was, to them, a mark of their calling and, as such, was respectable.

They sat around the table while I helped Mama carry in steaming platters of fried chicken, an enormous bowl of mashed potatoes, great quantities of gravy, steamed peas, and mounds of fresh sliced bread. The food disappeared more quickly than we could have imagined. Put to its task, the cook stove continued to pour out the heat that cooked our food and made the kitchen unbearably warm.

Mama and I felt secure in the fact that these men, with straw poking out of their hair in places, would bring home to their wives a glowing report of the feast they had enjoyed. The serving bowls were passed again and again while food found its way to the men's plates. With foresight, we had put away a few pieces of chicken and a smidgen of the other foods for us to eat when we could allow the time.

The huge meal was followed by lemon pie Mama had made that morning. It vanished as quickly as the other food. Pitchers of lemonade, considered too much of a luxury at other times, and coffee refills, Invited extravagant compliments.

All of the men, as they left the table, took time to thank Mama.   Rough looking though they were, paying respects held importance to them. It was part of the threshing tradition.

By the middle of the afternoon, the grain was nearly all threshed. Then, a sudden silence struck the farmyard. The big steam rig stopped. In the house we froze into inactivity. What if? What If the job could not be completed?.

We breathed an enormous sigh of relief when the steam engine coughed and seemed to swallow. It resumed activity and the men called on a hidden store of energy. No one minded the heat now. The tired limbs became reinvigorated. They would be able to finish this job after all. Men joked and laughed. The next farmer scheduled for threshers knew the rig and the farmers would move to his place. Men began going home. But the last formality was one huge blast of the steam whistle before the outfit pulled away.

Chickens flew out of the chicken coop. The dog barked furiously, then hid under the porch for the rest of the day. Our horse, Thor, raced down the lane at top speed, his fetlocks flying.

Threshing was over, but only until next year.

§§§

fourteen

THE RIGHTS OF WOMEN

My mother ventured bravely down the road;
It was her "first-time-driving" episode.

The Nineteenth Amendment to the constitution had come through a few years of American life. Yet, the fact that women could vote merely meant, in some cases, that men felt it necessary to keep female family members under close watch. It would not do to let them have much liberty too soon. And, to tell you the truth, women tasted their liberties carefully. Trying such reckless new activities as voting was not a thing anyone hurried into.

The same caution applied to the use of autos. Henry Ford's cars had become common on the roads in the 1930's. Still in rural areas, people parted reluctantly with their horses that were, literally, a part of the family. Transition from one mode of transportation to the other took place at a gradual rate.

The useful nature of automobiles had caught on; a person could drive into town, transact any necessary business and be back again, all within two hours' time. It would be ridiculous to argue the practicality. Papa bought a car and took to the roads along with millions of others. Then, he saw that it might be good for Mama to learn how to drive.

So, when Papa decided that Mama should learn the art of guiding an automobile along the roads, I hardly knew what attitude to take. Should I be joyful? Should I be sad? Should I be strictly neutral? With Papa as her instructor, Mama learned the art of driving an auto and practiced on the uneven acres of our farm.

One morning, Papa announced "Mama is going to drive to town today." Our breakfast conversation stopped. This was clearly a momentous event.

"Please go to the henhouse and pick up the eggs. I'll be taking them with me to town," Mama said. I went off to the assigned task too stunned to even relish, as I usually did, the warmth of the eggs taken from under the hens' bodies.

After the eggs were cleaned and put into the case, I washed the breakfast dishes. Mama changed into dressier clothes, and prepared to leave. It was a moment to be remembered. Papa, himself, lifted the egg crates into the back seat of the car. He issued the last minute instructions to Mama. She nodded, but said nothing more.

I noticed that she had crimped her brown hair with the curling iron, and pinched her cheeks to make them bloom. With Papa's help she cranked up the car, got inside, and drove away.

I resisted the temptation to stand by the mailbox, looking southward toward Mora, watching and waving until the car disappeared from view. I wanted to be as mature about this change as possible.

Mama left at ten thirty a.m. By eleven thirty Papa made frequent trips to the mailbox where he stood tall and lean, tipping the brim of his hat to shade his eyes. Intently, he studied the road to where it disappeared beyond the long hill south of us. I resisted the temptation to comment.

58

Numerous times, I remembered, Mama had stood at the window watching that same hill for signs of Papa's return from town. By reputation, sometimes he was delayed. Mama then usually turned her attention to the Christmas cactus on its stand by the window. She picked off imaginary bugs, and felt the soil for the fifteenth time.

The tables were turned, and the Nineteenth Amendment to the Constitution, giving women the right to vote, had started it.

Yes, now Papa was watching for Mama. He took his watch out of his pocket, studied it carefully, and put it back again, soon to repeat the process.

With some sympathy for Papa's having become the one to wait, I made a sandwich and put it before him, but he did not eat it. I filled his coffee cup with freshly cooked coffee, but he didn't touch it.

Ah! He walked restlessly into the living room to look down the road, and this time it paid off. He saw a car that looked familiar.

Papa made no pretenses now. He ran outside and stood by the mailbox. Here came Mama, the car half-hidden in a cloud of dust. The Model-T put-putted along at a snappy rate. *I'll bet those isinglass windows are really flapping now,* I thought.

Before Mama turned into our driveway, Papa began to look concerned, for she had scarcely reduced her speed. Still coming at a snappy rate, she approached the driveway. Papa fidgeted nervously.

Now, Mama looked neither to the right nor the left. Her whole attention was fixed on getting the car back successfully. She rounded the driveway at full speed, spitting gravel from the tires, and came onward through the yard with no regard for the chickens meandering here and there.

59

Papa was downright worried. He went to the back yard and stood beside the open doors to the cellar entrance. He took off his hat and waved, at whom and for what reason was not clear. "No, no Gertie," he shouted. I realized then, the serious nature of this situation. Papa only called our Mama "Gertie" in times of real distress.

Papa stood his ground; I'll say that for him. Waving his hat he still shouted "No, Gertie, No!" Chickens flew around in a shower of feathers. Mama pulled up to within six inches of the open cellar door, stopped the car and got out. Beaming at her audience, she said "Hi!"

I never knew all that took place. Mama was back with as much of the egg money as she could salvage. The car was unharmed. Papa put his hat on again, shook his head dazedly, and headed for the fields.

As for Mama, she showed me her purchase. Rickrack, lots of it. In fact, it looked like miles of rickrack
for trimming new aprons. While I could not imagine her making so many aprons, I did not say so.

She warmed up the coffee. As she worked around the kitchen, she hummed:

> This is my father's world,
> Why should my heart be sad?
> The Lord is King, let the heavens ring;
> God reigns, let the Earth be glad.

All was normal. But, it would never be the same again. Mama, freed by changes in the world, voted in the next election..

Why she even spent some of her egg money on a tube of lipstick the next time she went to town!

fifteen

THE WASHDAY

Washing our cloths required endless time;
We scrubbed away all traces of the grime.

Rural homes will soon be run by electricity," That was the caption of an article in our local paper. It seemed like fairyland dreams – when I was cold, I dreamed of fleecy robes. When I felt too warm, I dreamed of fans cooling my flesh.

But this was real. The year was 1938, and you could read in the newspaper about plans for electrification. It was part of the National Relief Act begun at the national level and trickling on down to local efforts.

Plans were actually in motion to cover the countryside with wires transmitting current to anyone who wanted it.

I looked at the electrical fixtures in Sears and Wards mail order catalogs with renewed interest. In fact, I dared to dream about a chandelier for our dining room. How pleased our Grandfather Olaf would have been!

In the meantime, we managed our laundry in the way it had always been done. Stacks of soiled clothing on the floor called for immediate action. I put away the catalogs and helped Mama repeat our same old process.

It was a cumbersome procedure. We carried in pail after pail of water which we pumped by hand. I helped, always fearful of spilling, for the pails were heavy. Some of the water filled the boiler set on the kitchen stovetop. Then we fed wood into the stove until we had a lively fire.

That in itself was a possible source of problems. A hot blaze over an extended time increased the risk of chimney fire. Our eyes, out of habit, followed a short section of stovepipe extending beyond the length that served the stove and fitting into the chimney. If that became red hot, as sometimes happened, we were in trouble.

Getting such a fire under control could be difficult. If it became an emergency, we threw sulfur into the firebox to smother the flames. I felt real fear at such times.

House fires were not uncommon to the area. Since we lived some distance from help of any kind, that was always a threat, and our hand pump brought up the only water available to fight it. Further, there was no way to control a wood fire.

After the danger passed, we proceeded again, for laundry was an all day matter. We dipped hot water from the boiler into the washer, which was originally a hand-operated contraption. At a later date, a small gas engine converted the washer into the closest thing to power-operated that we knew.

With the machine in operation, we set up the remaining equipment. A hand-operated wringer was fastened on the machine. The wringer fed its clothes into a tub for a second rinsing.

During full operation, another boiler of water stood heating on the stove. I used to watch with fascination as Mama peeled slices of FelsNaptha bar soap into the boiler. (This no doubt preceded other forms of soap; i.e., powdered and/or liquid.) We used to put hot suds in the boiler for boiling the dirtiest, most stubborn articles, whatever they might be. This was a long tiresome job that kept the stovetop covered for most of the day.

In addition to all of these operations, Mama had some clothing she scrubbed by hand on a scrubbing board. She rubbed soap generously over these items, working them against the board and also scrubbing them with a hand brush. While these operations were brutally hard work, they accomplished miracles with badly soiled pieces of clothing.

For the benefit of white articles, i.e., bed clothing, etcetera, we added bluing to the water. We expected it to accomplish what bleach does today. We had to measure it carefully, as too much bluing would leave tell-tale blue marks.

In the meantime, we operated the washing machine. Its dasher made a sloshing noise as it whipped the clothes around. Our chiming wall clock in the kitchen timed the operation.

When the rinse water became too sudsy, we dumped that out, carried in fresh pails of water, and continued the process. All of this had to be accomplished with the greatest care possible when outside temperatures were frigid. We dumped the water far enough from the house to eliminate the danger of our slipping on its frozen surface and to keep it away from garden areas that could be harmed by soapsuds.

While the stove carried out its purpose of heating water, the windows of the house became steamed over. Rivulets of moisture trickled down the panes. To me, this was the bleakest part of the process. The second bleakest was that I was expected to stand by as a helper.

I looked longingly at the book I was currently reading. It probably told about Miles Standish's courtship of Priscilla Alden. I knew better than to pick it up at such a crucial time. I felt like a prisoner in a house with weepy windows.

At intervals, we took a basket of clothes outside and hung the items on the line. In the severest cold, there was no more miserable job. I hardly had a piece on the line before it froze. Underwear, especially, froze into grotesque shapes.

I giggled often, being careful not to let anyone see me. I didn't want to be considered disrespectful, but all the same, a man's underwear stiffened into the shape of a person hugging himself was comical to look at.

The day drew to a close. By a process of draining the water into pails, we emptied the washer and the tubs. The paraphernalia was wheeled into the back porch, and the kitchen became neat and orderly. We had survived another washday.

Drying the clothes followed as another phase of the operation. Their stint on the line only partially dried them. We pulled out the drying racks and set them as close to one of the stoves as possible. Stockings, especially, demanded immediate attention.

We hung them on the nickel-plated fenders of the big heating stove in the living room. That required close attention, lest they scorch there. A snapping fire in the stove offered pleasant company but presented a hazard. We kept under close watch anything that was drying near the stoves.

When washday was over, I felt tremendous relief. A celebration was due. Once again, we had clean clothing, bed sheets, towels and all of the pieces of equipment that keep a household running.

So far, electricity was only a promise on the horizon, much like a cloud that might or might not produce needed rain.

§§§

THE NEIGHBORS

I followed the ruts, that marked the bumpy way,
Up to the neighbor's farm place, on that day.

White clouds bounced along the heavens as if they were driven by our dog Hero when he herded the cattle. In my mind, I carried a message to a neighbor, but my right hand was tightened to a fist as if I were holding it. My errand caused me to feel a bit anxious - - I wanted so much to do it right.

A lot of rain had fallen in early spring months. "Good for the crops," I heard my parents say. I did not doubt that for a moment, but those same rain showers made the road a mass of muck. Tire tracks from cars crisscrossed each other. Here and there I could see the narrower ridges of wagon wheels and the unmistakable imprints of horses' hooves. The roadbed had dried since the last shower. Tracks of autos that passed this way crisscrossed each other back and forth. I followed a rut for several feet before it seemed to disappear, and then I looked for another.

My attention settled on a plump yellow bumblebee feeding on the clover growing at roadside. I could hear the song of a meadowlark from the meadow south of the house. But, I knew I must remember the message I had been sent to deliver. "We would like to pick the crab apples off that tree that stands by the Lutheran cemetery if it's all right with you. Last year we noticed they fell and went to waste."

The message could have been delivered by telephone, except that Papa had never become comfortable talking on the phone. So, I was selected to deliver the massage by hand. That was a matter of dispute, too, since some of my siblings wanted to go along. I was not without fault. A walk by myself was a chance to release my imagination. For that reason, I rejected their company. Make-believe companions walked the same speed I walked. They didn't talk all of the time, either.

Now, I had nothing to do but walk in the rut I tried to follow except that sometimes it disappeared into another rut. I pretended it led to an enchanted castle and, soon, I would meet the princess who lived there.

Sounds of a car motor broke my reverie. I looked behind and saw a Model-A Ford bou0ncing along the bumpy road. Following instructions from Mama and Papa, I stepped down into the ditch as the car approached. The car stopped. "Hello!" the driver said. "You one of Herman's girls?" I nodded, unable to think of anything else to say. The man laughed. He reached into his pocket. "Here," he said holding something in his fingers. I stepped up, and took what he had handed me. He gave a funny little salute and drove away. "Wow!" I said. He had given me a nickel. I thought even pennies were generous. I wondered if I should have kept the nickel. What would Mama and Papa say?

Once again, I found a rut to walk in. I heard a humming noise and looked upward at the telephone lines with those funny little blue insulators strung on the wires. On cold winter days when we walked to school the insulators hummed more loudly than now. I wondered why?

As I approached the neighbor's place it was time for my next worry. *"Will their dog come running out to bark at me?"* My stomach flopped over at the thought. Although I didn't know if their dog was mean, it could be true. This time I didn't need to worry. One of the men who lived there came to meet me in the driveway. "Hello," he said. "Yew coming to see us?"

Now my sense of obligation overcame my bashfulness. "I came to ask something." No sense in telling it all at once. The neighbor might ask me in the house. I had heard they baked a lot of goodies.

"Awright," the man said. They spoke Norwegian at home and used English only when they spoke to others. When my cousin imitated speech like this, we thought it was funny.

The man brought me into the house. A woman there had lots of smiles. She led me carefully through the kitchen to the table, almost as if she were afraid I would break if I didn't have help. I felt bashful, but it was good to feel special.

"Now, vat did yew come to say?" The man asked.

The woman put a plate of cookies on the table. They were sprinkled with sugar. My mouth watered, but I didn't touch them. First, I had to give the people my message about picking the apples. It came out in a rush. When I finished I reached for a cookie.

The man thought for a moment. "Yah!" He said. He looked at the woman who nodded. "Dey don't belong to us, but a man who owns dem is gone for a while. I t'ink its awright."

"Tell Herman," the man began. "Vell, tell your Papa dat I call him on da phone. Is it two short rings and a long?"

I nodded, for that was our ring on the party line

and, then, they talked to me about other things - - about school - -about helping at home - - about the river.

"Don't you have a river?" I asked when they said no, I felt surprised. *What on earth did people do without a river?* Then, I remembered they had a windmill and a big tank holding water beside the barn.

I knew it was time to go. They stood aside as I walked away. "Goodbye!" they called.

Before reaching the road, I realized that I had not seen the dog. I felt foolish knowing I had been scared about something that didn't happen.

On the way back, I felt lighthearted enough to skip a few steps. The meadowlark was still singing, and his song seemed to be my song.

A car came from the hill to the south. Again, I stepped aside. The driver stopped, too. "Hullo!" the man shouted. It was our neighbor to the west. He talked a little about its being a nice day. Then he started away. "Goodbye, Powder Face," He yelled with a little wave of his hand.

I felt a warm flush over my cheeks. It was his way of teasing me about my skin and my hair.

I was proud to go back home with a message. "Mr. G- - will call you."

Proud and giggling, too, because I knew Papa's yelling into the phone would not make his message any easier to understand.

Now that I had accomplished my errand, my mind raced ahead. I wanted so much to do the errand well. My mind hurried the way our horse, Thor, .galloped for no reason at all. I liked watching him race across the pastures with his black mane flying and his hooves raising dust from bare places in the lane.

69

One more detail of my growing up on the farm had taken place. I savored anything that made me feel more grown up. I hoped to get a passing score for this errand n the same way I strived for passing grades in school. My Grandpa Nub always said, "You must work hard and get good marks."

The road with its deep ruts which I had followed would become smooth in the future. Still, it was more dangerous because of increased traffic. And, the travelers would be strangers. Imagine! Strangers on this road with grassy ditches on each side where wild roses bloomed and the sweetest berries imaginable grew.

§§§

seventeen

THE HOUSE

Two stories high, the house looked to the west,
Too modest to lay claim to being best.

As I came walking home from school, I looked toward the house with a spiral of smoke curling out of its chimney. And, I began the singsong chant that had been haunting me. At school we learned: This is the house that Jack built. I was captured by the music in the repetitive lines, but I changed the words:

This is the farmer sowing the corn,
That kept the cock that crowed in the morn,
That cut down the trees to get the wood . . ."

But the lines always ended with, "This is the house that Grandfather Olaf built."

It was my delicious secret. When I carried wood to the house, when I went to get pails of water, when I went to get eggs from the henhouse, I used the chant to divert my mind - - "This is the house that Grandfather Olaf built."

I knew that he had planned the house in every detail, including the wood box in the chimney corner where you could get warm in the coldest weather. He had planned the cellar below the frame building and its high-peaked roof that accommodated a full second floor. He had drawn into his plans a window in the second floor hallway from which I could see the shiny ribbon that was the Knife River wending its way to join the Snake River in Mora.

Grandfather Olaf knew this house the way I knew it. He had chosen the lumber throughout and planned the plastering of inside walls. He decided the dimensions of the big, high-ceilinged living room. With forethought, he had built the outside entrance to the cellar on the east side of the house, away from the strongest winds.

Grandfather Olaf had planned that the fields would stand in the forefront, laid out with the far-seeing eye of a man who maps his own destiny, but asks for God's blessing. He walked along the river before buying the land, and he must have found the low place by the water's edge where the dragonflies darted back and forth before I breathed my first breath.

In the house's living room, under the watchful eyes of Olaf and Anna from their portraits on the wall, we consecrated the high-ceilinged room in our own way. Guided by music from the organ, we sang the same hymns as those pouring forth from the church that Olaf decreed-to-be-built. Into that living room, we wove our own family traditions that Olaf would have approved.

When we lifted down the family portraits before fresh wallpaper was hung, we covered those pictures with care. Their portraits could never be made again, for Olaf and Anna had gone to answer God's call.

From the upstairs window on the west, I - - Olaf's Granddaughter - - drank in the view. From that height, I could see a long distance. In summertime, I saw acres of clover bending obediently to the winds. In the wintertime, I saw the vast field with a snow covering that caught afire with brilliance under a wintry sun.

Under Grandfather Olaf's supervision, a carved rosette adorned the upper corners of every doorway in the house. They added a detail of elegance to plain features that might have been considered austere.

We often had dinner guests whom we entertained in the generous dining room that came alive out of Grandfather Olaf's planning. In that same room, in time, a radio spoke to us from a table in the corner. From that place, in the house that Olaf built, a new script of living included us in its future. From that room, we - - the second generation of Swedish Americans - - found ourselves drawn into the outside world.

Olaf's blueprints - - although they may not have been called that then - - included dimensions for a generous-sized kitchen. Three windows on the west framed a snow scene in winter. The disappearing sun glazed the field so that it looked like a path inlaid with diamonds.

This is the house that Grandfather Olaf built. The four-paneled painted doors served us well for a lifetime beyond his. The pantry offered its shelves for the pies and cakes, doughnuts, bread, pies and, oh yes, cream puffs that provoked great interest at the same round dining room table that Olaf had used.

When the siding needed replacing, an asbestos siding took its place. It hardly did justice to the house that Olaf built. But, the front porch smiled its hospitality on the people passing by for another half-century.

Now, strangers pull shades over the windows at night. Strangers listen in summer from the back porch door for the music of crickets and the low hum of the river. Strangers take one last look before closing up the house to see if the Northern Lights are active.

The house that Grandfather Olaf built has a hallowed place in memory. The beveled rosettes around each door may still be there. The stairway to the second floor still climbs up for twenty-three steps and maybe the thirteenth step still squeaks.

The front door of the house is still open to guests although, "Valkommen" may be spoken in another way. The place is almost impervious to wear, to fire, to storm damage. It will always stand there for his descendants, for this is the house that Grandfather Olaf built.

§§§

eighteen

THE TEAKETTLE

A smoldering fire in the stove would be
Enough to keep the kettle bubbling cheerfully.

I opened the back door of our house and walked into the kitchen. The teakettle gasped faintly from its perch on the cook stove where a fire smoldered. How good were the prospects for a cup of freshly cooked coffee for Mama and Papa, as well as visitors who stopped by?

We had been trained in the ways of our times, and we knew how to produce a hotbed of coals, the beginnings of a fire that snapped with vigor. A fire that could bristle with energy. A fire that devoured sticks of wood.

Even if there had been no refueling and nothing more survived than a spark, hot ashes would keep water in the reservoir warm. If I filled some into the teakettle, we would have percolating action in no time at all. A few sticks of dry wood spurred the effort.

In no time at all, heat radiated from the stove's surface. Mama sometimes tested it with water. When drops danced across the stove's metal expanse, conditions were good for cooking coffee.

We learned other little tricks, too. So much of life revolved around drinking coffee, our chief social beverage. If waiting for the coffee tried the patience of some, we might put out a plate of jelly roll slices. They looked pretty, especially on a white plate, and they seemed to promise satisfaction.

When the teakettle we had used for years sprung a leak, it was something of a crisis, although it was not a recent development. Over the years leaks had appeared at frequent intervals. Papa was summoned, then, with a soldering iron and solder; over and over again, he used the same treatment. Each time the kettle became heavier. It had finally become too heavy to lift. A teakettle beyond recall.

This called for action and we decided to go to an auction sale held that day. Auction sales, besides being a practical matter, brought neighbors, relatives, and friends together. They could visit over cups of coffee. Excitement built up at this sale as the auctioneer brought the bidding up to a lively pitch. To our joy, he held up a copper teakettle. "Here we are, folks!" he chanted. "A quarter? Fifty cents? Will you give me seventy-five?"

"One dollar," Papa shouted with only a small quaver in his voice to show nervousness over speaking out so boldly in a public place.

There were no other bids. "One dollar, then," the auctioneer replied and a helper brought the teakettle to Papa in a paper bag.

After we got the teakettle home, we examined it carefully. One small dent near the seam of the kettle hardly showed. But, would it hold water? We tested it. We found no leaks.

After Mama washed it in warm soapsuds and rinsed it several times, we put the teakettle on the cook stove. Shortly afterward we heard a low humming noise. The voice of the teakettle! Not until later did we discover its whistling ability. Just imagine!

We admired its copper body, its curved handle ending in a carved wooden piece at the top. We gathered around it to get full benefit of its appearance.

Mama exclaimed, "My! Isn't that something?" That said it for all of us.

It held three quarts of water (well, maybe two and a half). We filled its rotund body before setting it on the stove where it resided ever after. After each meal, we removed it from the stove and wiped its chubby body free of frying pan splatters.

We followed its operation with interest from the first time it heated water for us, gurgling and sputtering, until later when it became an old friend of ours. It nursed us through hard times. When a late frost killed the garden plants shortly after they emerged, green and full of vitality, we went for comfort to the copper teakettle. We blew on dying embers in the firebox to encourage a talkative fire.

We gathered around the kitchen table, waiting for the teakettle to do its work. Mama knew an opportunity when she saw one. In this case she took a knife and lopped off pieces from a loaf of bread she had set aside to rise.

She kneaded the pieces into small flat cakes which she laid on the stovetop for a few seconds where they continued to rise and bake. As soon as one was finished, Mama slathered it with good butter and jam or cheese. One by one, she served each of us this warm, tasty kind of biscuit.

Accompanied by coffee or cocoa, it couldn't be beat. By this time, hot water found its way into the coffee pot and the aroma of coffee filled our kitchen.

One day, the kettle began issuing choppy little noises. I stopped to listen. "Ah," I said. "Do you hear that? Our teakettle has the hiccups."

Sometimes guests stayed to hear the hiccups. The teakettle became a featured performer.

If we should leave the teakettle on when the fire was pushed to the limit for some occasion, the vessel fairly danced. Its cover shuttled up and down. Steam escaped from it in cheery puffs. It might stop visitors in their tracks.

As a companion, its value was unmistakable. While it gurgled on the stove, emitting little toots of pleasure, I hummed while dusting the furniture. - - I sang softly even while cleaning up the cream separator, a job I despised. I did a quick two-step as I picked up fallen leaves from the Christmas cactus and the geraniums.

Something stirred within me when I entered the kitchen. I heard the voice of the teakettle; raspy at times, but always conversational.

That teakettle of ours could hum and whistle as well as heat water. What a shame it would have been if we had not allowed it to become something more than a mere object in our possession.

§§§

nineteen

THE KITCHEN RANGE

Just a chunk of metal, you might say,
But it kept the embers glowing night and day.

To me, the range watched over the kitchen in a pleasing way. When fire burned in the stove, my hopes for a meal became warm, too. I drew near the stove either for its beverages, cocoa for the kids or coffee for the grownups, or to be with others who had needs similar to mine.

And, what about late in the evening, when everyone else had gone to bed? I could sit and read with my feet in the toasty warm oven. That was a luxury I enjoyed.

Probably, the reservoir out-classed all other features on the kitchen range. It was roughly twenty inches wide, measuring thirty inches from the front to the back. It kept water warm for washing hands, for filling the teakettle, for washing dishes, and for cooking.

Nothing about it seemed to spell "danger." But, one day, Mama baked a sponge cake. It rose upward, golden and tempting. The next step would be icing.

Someone called to Mama as she stood with the cake in her hand after it was removed from the pan. With a quick flip she dropped the cake into the reservoir full of water. She cried out, her cry seeming to fill the room.

Not only did we lose the cake, gone beyond recall, but the water had to be dipped out and carried away. Then we brought in clean water for a fresh start.

Sometimes the stove top became littered with wood chips and even bits of fried egg. That brought on a cleaning siege. Worst of all, the stove must be cold before the inky black cleaning solution could be applied.

I hated such times. Mama became a demon of perfection, applying the solution with a generous hand. But when the job was finished, and the stove stood in its place looking like an ebony god, I felt proud.

Across the top of the stove, warming ovens jutted outward. A rounded cover, lavishly trimmed with shiny nickel, moved up and down. Inside, a shelf provided room for storage.

While that was a handy feature, it had a down side. Leftover pancakes stored there might stay a few days before being discovered. A household rule decreed that the one who found them must dispose of them. We did so, complaining bitterly.

Although the kitchen range stood near the chimney, it had an interesting array of stovepipes. They began at the top of the range, rose a few feet straight upward, made a sharp jog, and then continued on into a curving pipe with an extension that fit the chimney opening.

A screw-like handle projecting outward controlled the flue that directed the smoke toward the chimney. If the wind changed direction, you would probably want to make an adjustment.

When the wind was in the east, the flue chattered like a talkative person. In the early morning, I liked to lie in bed for a while after waking up. While

Papa got the house warm and put on the coffee pot, the flue carried on a lively commentary.

Once, the stove became the center of a mishap. During an early December cold spell Papa worked at the woodpile outside. We expected him to keep at this task for the rest of the day.

A man who was once a neighbor drove into the yard. He and Papa visited outside for a while. But, apparently, they found more to say, and came into the house for a cup of coffee and some of Mama's baked goods.

We had interrupted our work inside to indulge in a songfest. One of my sisters played the organ. We all sang with her. It was close enough to Christmas to make singing carols the right thing to do. How we enjoyed ourselves!

But then Papa burst into the room. "Gertie!" "Gertie" he cried. Our songfest came to an abrupt stop. "Gertie!" Papa said, in a shocked tone. "The fire has gone out!"

We scattered to various parts of the house. Such neglect was never heard of before. The kitchen fire had burned out and there was no hot coffee!

A great fuss and clamor followed. I was dispatched to the woodpile to find some pieces of kindling wood. Then, Mama got a lively fire going. Fortunately, the kindling snapped and crackled when it took fire, a clear sign of encouragement. Soon, hot coffee was ready, and the grownups visited and lunched on coffee cake with slices of Land 'O' Lakes cheese.

The kitchen range provided a big oven. In fact there was room in it for a half dozen single loaf tins of bread side by side. Because of its insulation, those loaves left the oven browned and baked to perfection.

During the baking process, a heavenly scent of baking bread floated through our two-story house. It escaped via doorways and found its way into upstairs bedrooms. It reminded us that if we wanted "the heel" we had better make our claim soon. And, if one of us got angry and threatened to leave home, it would not be on bread-baking day.

None of its attractive features, for my personal taste, was greater than the nickel lettering on the front of the oven door. It spelled out "Adirondack." Often, I stooped down to trace the elegant swirls with my fingers.

I saw the name spelling the place where the stove had come from. A far away place, I felt sure. Some place with tall buildings, with street sellers playing their hurdy-gurdies, and with hawkers crying "Extra, extra. Read all about it!"

The top of our stove, a wide expanse of cast iron, offered space for a half dozen removable lids. In the surface of each lid, there was a groove that a handle fit into. We could remove that lid when we wanted to add more wood.

On one side, a big, hinged, lid could be lifted to permit adding larger pieces of wood. That was a handy feature except that everything on the surface had to be taken off; the teakettle, the coffee pot, or the cooking kettles.

Across that same field of iron, Mama processed her lefse, the Norwegian bread that highlighted our holiday season. I watched with interest as she picked up a piece of the dough made of potatoes, flour and milk. The piece was roughly the size of a child's fist.

Mama kneaded that piece thoroughly, moving it from one hand to the other. Then came the part I liked to watch. She rolled it into a circular shape about

22 inches in diameter. Next, she slid the carved wooden turner underneath, draped the lefse over it and approached the hot stove.

She put the lefse on the surface and left it there for a few seconds. After it was turned, I saw that the bread bore brownish splotches. It looked to me, for all the world, like my father's Guernsey cows.

From lefse to delectable coffee cakes, to sponge and angel food cakes, our oven turned out an enviable quantity of baked goods. As one of Mama's daughter's I was "in training" from the time I was a little girl until I left home. It would never do to betray our early training in Mama's kitchen on the majestic monarch wood-burning range.

It is well that I never found out the stove really came from Detroit, Michigan or some place like Minnesota. Our kitchen range deserved, I thought, the most romantic of histories.

The stove brought into our kitchen the clamor of steel mills, the technical touches of skilled workers, and a long voyage over a railway whose trestles swayed above deep gullies and rivulets.

It was our unmatched Monarch Of The Kitchen.

§§§

twenty

THE CLAW-LEGGED KITCHEN TABLE

We gathered there together every day,
To eat, and play and sometimes talk, and pray.

Flanked by narrow, double hung windows on the north, the claw-legged kitchen table faced another pair of windows on the west. Like an idol of heroic proportions, it occupied the center of the room. It was sturdy and old - - like a good teacher in its way.

I dropped my books there when I came home from school. They would have to be moved later but they presently looked out from a place on the table. A necessary stop, that place was the area from which all traffic funneled in other directions.

Since our kitchen did not boast of working surface on the cupboard, my mother kneaded her bread dough on the table. The loaves she shaped rose to plump perfection. She set them in temporary spots and, after covering the table, put the loaves there to rise.

We worked our school lessons at the kitchen table. I recall taking off the cloth cover so that our pencils would not stumble on wrinkles. The surface of the table, however, had its own grooves and bumpy places.

Many years passed before I realized that continued use of objects can make them dear. Now, I regret disposing of some items too quickly. If kept longer they might have garnered more value, as did the old claw-legged kitchen table.

I can thank that kitchen table at home for a lesson I learned in cleanliness. Its grooved, claw legs required cleaning on Saturday mornings. When it was my turn, I felt rebellious. *Who will ever know I've done this?* I stormed.

"Clean places do not invite inspection," I was told. "Only when a job is unfinished, do prying eyes find it."

Since then I have often wished that my human mistakes could be scraped out of existence like the dirt in those grooved table legs.

More than once I objected to that table. I thought it was too big, its clawed feet clumsy, and the gouges in its surface disgusting.

That was before I realized continued use of things makes them dear.

We always met around that table for our meals. We met when happiness provided an aura of plenty around us. We felt in harmony with each other and gratitude came easily. We met in times of strained relationships when gloom required a place setting of its own, because it took on an almost physical form.

The undeniable fact is that each of us had a place at the table. I remember sitting opposite Mama. I found security in the fact that my place stood empty unless I was there.

The table was the hub of activity during canning season. We peeled and quartered tomatoes, packing them into jars and getting them ready for the hot bath. And then, at last, we set the jars on the table's surface to cool. There the light from the west window highlighted their orange-red color.

But, our kitchen table was at its best after the evening meal. It invited the activities of a family, such as, playing games or reading books. "Come, sit at my side," it seemed to say to my mother with her handwork.

The table's use became enhanced when a group gathered around it. As with a person who has God at his center, a spirit of acceptance seemed to flow outward.

It is a mistake, I realized some time ago, to get rid of objects too quickly. If kept longer, they might have acquired the same value as the old claw-legged kitchen table. The chipped surface of that table returns in memory with a patina of everlasting polish.

§§§

twenty one

THE CHIMNEY CORNER SPY

All traffic through the household passed me by,
I was the shameless chimney corner spy.

W hat are you doing down there?" Mama
asked me when she found me scrunched
down behind the stove. I hardly knew
what to say. This was a hiding place during my
childhood; my retreat from reality. The wood elves
that appeared whenever I looked for them gathered
like happy thoughts in this place.

"I like it here, because it's warm and cozy." I
replied. To my right the wood box kept its bounty
near at hand. And, at right angles to the chimney,
bricks mounted in their pattern, up, up and up all the
way to the roof. The chimney bricks threw off warmth
even when the fire had burned down to embers.

Mama went off to other issues, and I was alone
to listen to the occasional sparks in the firebox of the
stove. When a lively fire burned, I often heard showers
of sparks. Sometimes they sounded like midget
explosions. It depended on the kind of wood being
burned. I tried to guess what was burning at the
present time.

If the wood had not dried out, I could hear a
slow sizzle. While that did not produce a hot enough
fire for cooking, it sounded interesting. I knew,
however, that someone would discover the green
wood. At mealtime, we could not tolerate such

ineffective fuel. It would probably be removed from the firebox, tossed outside on the ash pile, and replaced with wood that caught fire quickly, and started a leaping blaze.

Soon the teakettle would hum cheerfully, and prospects for a meal improved. With so much activity in the immediate area, I left my hiding place behind the stove. Beside, if someone discovered me, I would be sent on an errand.

I returned to my hiding place behind the stove whenever possible. Strange items turned up there: a pair of pliers I knew Papa had been searching for - - and which had been put there with his wet mittens, only to slide under an errant potholder. Mama's wooden darning egg that had been missing for days and had apparently rolled out of her mending basket. And the clamp that tightened fruit jar lids which someone put down for a moment and forgot. I used all the tact I could muster when I found such things, because I knew no one liked to own up to having misplaced them.

Sometimes it was not prudent to own up to having found them until several days had passed. At other times, I became the heroine by producing them when needed, seemingly, out of nowhere.

For all the convenience of having these items appear, I noticed that popularity with my siblings declined correspondingly, for heroism went unappreciated. Life could be hard to figure out!

I liked the smell of the chimney corner - - the combinations of wood and smoke and sometimes the resin that oozed out of the green pine. The tangy fragrance of burning birch bark that lingered in the vicinity. Of course there were cooking smells, too, that did not vanish right away.

Smoked pork - - or ham - - left a sharp, lasting smell. It invaded the chimney corner. I could not sit there if I felt hungry, and had to wait for our evening meal. The fragrances found me and held me captive. I imagined they had shapes like curling smoke, billowing out and, then, finally, drifting to nothing.

The surface of the wall covering behind the stove was shiny, reputed to be a non-burnable substance. When it was new it looked glossy, but gradually, it acquired spatters of grease that formed patterns of their own and did not wash out easily.

The chimney corner, aside from its being my chosen places became a kind of refuge. Wet gloves, mittens, scarves and even gunny sacks dried out there. A wet jacket might hang over the corner of the wood box until its moisture baked away.

Once.,a brooding hen hatched her chicks early in April. Mama found them in the haymow. Since the weather was still cold, those tiny, fluffy, peepy chicks might have been frozen stiff.

So, Mama made a home for them in an empty grocery box. They peep-peeped through the days until they were big enough to survive. Enchanted, at first, I fussed over them which earned me sort of a custodial role. That was fun in the beginning but soon wore off, and I was horrified to find that I was stuck with the job of taking care of Mama's refugees.

The chimney corner had many possibilities. We could put a flat board over the wood box, thereby creating a surface on which dishes for supper could rest without cooling off completely. Old newspapers somehow found their way into the chimney corner, ostensibly, for fire-building but also as a convenient disposal.

Once the dog - - kept outside on the principle that dogs were not meant to be indoors - - came in to nurse a wounded paw. He soon found that his chosen habitat was the chimney corner. Getting him back outside required coaxing and when that failed, strong-arm tactics.

The chimney corner acquired the house's personality. Warm, inviting, a place of mysteries, it was a haven for body and soul.

The sleek functional designs of modern houses offer "class" in preference to comfort. But, where, in such elegant places can you find a haven like the chimney corner? What else can offer such comforts as the heat oozing out of a monstrous cast iron wood stove? What else dares to protrude in some areas and shelter hidden crannies in others? What else has the bald faced courage to preside over an area littered with wood chips and a film of ashes?

What else dares to shelter such warm memories?

§§§

twenty two

THE PANTRY

The tastiest of foods found refuge there,
Secure unless we sampled on a dare.

An angel food cake, tall and majestic looking was often the first thing you saw when you came into the pantry. It would have been frosted with Seven-Minute frosting made with egg-whites and sugar. It was crowned with the whiteness of the frosting. It was a test of endurance if you could go into the pantry and not be tempted to taste that cake standing there!

In addition to the angel food cake, I remember the big metal tin that rested on the floor. It held an estimated fifty pounds of flour used for baking and cooking. However careful we were when reaching into the tin, flour spilled on the floor to make a ring resembling the ring around the moon on a crisp, cold winter night.

We waged a constant war against that collection of flour on the floor, for it was an invitation to mice. Since the pantry shelves housed foodstuffs, we could not afford to tolerate the little creatures. Baiting traps and disposing of forlorn gray bodies became an almost daily job.

On the top shelf, in a modest unit, stood our half-dozen cookbooks. The one I remember best was Watkins. From that we chose our recipes for muffins and cakes. Most of the recipes called for two cups of flour, one cup of sugar and two eggs, plus whatever other ingredients were required.

With such unimaginative beginnings, we were hardly likely to come up with anything out-of-the-ordinary, but the recipes were at least, reliable. Along the margins of the books previous users had penned such warnings as "measure lightly on this one," Or perhaps, "this one falls if you don't beat the eggs long enough."

There was no door to the pantry. Its open doorway made easy access for the flow of traffic to and from the kitchen. It also contributed to an unforgettable incident.

One morning, while I was gathering the necessary ingredients for pancakes, I had a daring idea that prompted me to set the ingredients down. I had grown tall enough to hook my fingers over the door frame. The temptation to try a long jump was more than I could resist.

My first try was unsuccessful but, on the second try, I gave a wild whoop and swung into the middle of the kitchen. At that moment the door opened and admitted Papa with a full pail of milk. He looked at me with astonishment, and I realized I was standing in a half-crouched position. A painful blush made its way from my extremities to the top of my blonde head.

I hurried toward the dining room where I invented an errand until I could collect my senses again. But before leaving, I caught the smile Mama tried to hide.

You might say the pantry was the hub of all activity. While we mixed pancakes, cookies, cakes, breads, and other such bounty on the kitchen table, we collected everything we needed from the pantry.

In a bowl on the shelf in plain view stood the newly laid eggs we had collected from the henhouse - - cackle berries, Papa fondly called them.

All of the store-bought items, such as raisins, soda and graham crackers, were kept in the pantry. A big container of oatmeal stood in a handy position. Granulated, brown and powdered sugar stood their places on the shelves. The necessary crock of home-rendered lard held down a corner of the pantry shelf. On the floor, nestled in beside the flour bin, stood the gallon jar of molasses, considered as basic a product as sugar and flour.

The pantry had heavy usage. It was hard to keep clean, too, because of the activity there. Yet, Mama liked to keep it presentable.

And to that end, she bought yards of shelf paper. It was scalloped, usually with a floral pattern - - Sometimes roses, sometimes pansies. We were breathless over its beauty when that shelf paper was newly installed, thumb-tacked at six-to-eight-inch intervals.

I knew that I, for one, vowed I would never make a clumsy move that would tear that shelf paper. That did not last, of course. Inevitably, the first tear appeared. After that, other tears occurred with a rapidity rivaling that of a rain shower in April.

When the household was run in an orderly fashion, our cakes and pies resided on the pantry shelves. They looked resplendent there, and I sighed for the wonder of it all. Such an appearance of prosperity was almost more than one could stand.

There were loaves of sweetened bread rolled into wax paper and dish towels. There was a mound of freshly baked cookies, waiting to be stored into containers, but vanishing at an alarming rate before that ever happened. Sometimes, there was a high, regal-looking angel food cake to be kept for Sunday dinner.

The mouth-watering lusciousness of that cake's appearance was a threat to its ever lasting that long. It was made from a great aunt's never-failing recipe included herein.

<u>Family Angel Cake (Simply Good!)</u>
1   Cup sifted cake flour
¼   Teaspoon almond extract
1¼   Cup Sugar
1   Teaspoon cream of tartar
1   Cup egg whites (8-10 eggs)
½   Teaspoon salt
¼   Teaspoon vanilla

Sift ¼ cup sugar and flour together four times. Beat egg whites, cream of tartar and salt to a stiff form. Add remaining sugar, a little at a time, beating it in, preferably with a rotary beater. Add flavoring. Fold in flour, sifting it gradually over the egg white and sugar mixture. Pour into a large ungreased pan, cut through batter with a spatula to remove large air bubbles. Bake in a moderate oven (350˚ F) 45-60 minutes. Remove from oven, invert pan 1 hour.

§§§

twenty three
THE QUILT

Across the length and breadth of that percale,
Acres of flowers bloomed--as in a fairy tale.

S ave the scraps, we can use them for something." was repeated often in our day-to-day lives. In fact, you might say "Save the scraps" governed our behavior like a lesser law. A law handed from generation to generation.

Scraps in this case referred to cloth used for quilts. The "nice print dress" for which we purchased yard goods had secondary consideration. I longed for a dress made from flowered dimity. That was unlikely to ever happen, for dimity, as we knew it, was a cloth in which sheer strips alternated with heavier ones. The sheer strips make it unsuitable for quilts.

While I felt sad to realize I would probably never own a dimity dress, I also longed to see a piece in a finished quilt that matched something I wore. A harmless kind of vanity that makes some persons want to see a piece of themselves in other places to be appreciated.

As my maternal grandmother, Julia, and Mama bent their heads over the Sears and Wards catalogs, shopping for cotton by the yard, the word 'serviceable' threaded through their conversation. I despised the word. It meant corduroy for a skirt when I longed for velvet. It meant underclothing made of unbleached muslin when I waltzed through my days in slinky silk.

Saving the scraps was as directly related to making quilts as cutting hay was to filling the haymow. We knew the signs that foretold quilting without being informed. Mama, with a puckered forehead and humming a tuneless kind of song, began prowling in out-of-the-way places. From the corner of one closet she pulled a discarded flour sack pillowcase, stuffed with the remnants of yard goods.

She brought her treasures downstairs where she could work on them "when there was time." That didn't happen for a week or more. By then, Mama had pulled another pillowcase out of the closet area over the hidden stairs to the cellar.

This one bore a suspicious looking bulge on one side. The bulge was as fascinating to me as an unopened letter.

One day, a third pillowcase appeared. I did not see where Mama had found this one. Then I remembered a bunchy looking heap in the corner of the hall from which the stairway reached to our second floor. That heap vanished, and I never saw it again.

One evening after supper, and after the barn chores were completed, Mama, with some ceremony brought forth the three pillowcases. She pulled them up beside her chair. Leaning over, she opened up one pillowcase and drew out a piece of daintily flowered percale with ragged edges.

Light from the Coleman lamp poured forth its radiance on Mama's bent head. Some gray hair nestled among the strands of brown, and I wondered, with a feeling of foreboding, what they were doing there.

Mama began removing the scraps of leftover pieces of yard goods saved from the most recent sewing projects. I noticed a swatch of the material from which Mama made my sky-blue skirt. I had almost forgotten how grand it felt the first time I wore it. How it was cut a little wider, in fact, almost flared. If Mama could afford a bigger piece of percale, it would have been even wider.

When it was new, its hemline brushed my legs, filling me with an unfamiliar awareness of myself and what I wore. What a wonderful prize package rested there with other scraps!

Most of what Mama removed from their secret hiding places failed to interest me. But, at last, she pulled out the piece that had pushed against the side of the pillowcase.

It was a piece Mama bought for patching Papa's overalls. We called it overall-stuff. Someday it would be known as denim. From such lowly material, the fashion world produced highly desirable garments.

The pieces unearthed from their hiding places waited to be pressed flat. Flat irons made their way to the top of the kitchen range. We began the long process of pressing out each crumpled bit of cloth.

We entered the next stage of quilting.

This became sandwiched between washing and ironing clothes, cooking meals and washing dishes, cleaning out milk pails and parts of the cream separator, not to mention keeping an orderly house - - What an enormous job!

At last, the pieces were all pressed and piled in neat stacks. Mama had to find a place where they could rest undisturbed until they were used. One evening, she took a stack of scraps and went to the Singer sewing machine.

That piece of equipment held a kind of exalted place in our household. Partly because it performed a necessary function. Partly because it was trimmed and decorated to look nice. Underneath the head of the machine, an ornate structure held the machine together. A part of it dropped down to the pedal. Iron pieces worked into elegant scrolls and decorated with gold paint made the sewing machine look like a structure of art. We had no idea of the principle on which the machine worked. Mama learned about it in a gradual process as she tinkered with the parts and made discoveries about different stitches. The whir-r-r-r of the machine became a familiar sound in our kitchen. It was an industrious type of sound that brought a respect to the business of sewing that hand sewing never enjoyed.

The quilt that Mama launched on was to be a crazy quilt. This meant the pieces could be joined in a mosaic-like pattern. I thought, wistfully, of the beautiful patterned quilts she had made.

The fan quilt was on Mama and Papa's bed. Mama had started a butterfly quilt, but there was not enough time to finish it. I was twelve years old and insensitive, yet, to the quicksilver passage of time. I did not know that in hardly more than a decade, Mama's quilting projects would be put away forever.

But, now, with the pieces ironed flat, she held a swatch of material, envisioning the finished product. She hummed, and I knew she was ready to begin. Mama always hummed when she started a new project.

For days, she worked at her sewing machine in moments pruned from an endless list of chores. With deft hands, she tucked raw edges out of sight and anchored them in place. The finished parts already had a wild, jubilant sort of beauty.

A crazy quilt reflected the creative urges of its maker. Mama's became a work of art.

When, at last the pieces were sewed together, Mama placed a telephone call to someone in the neighborhood. A lady named Svea, who lived with her son, owned the quilting frames. Arrangements took place and Papa seized the opportunity to go and get them.

Papa possessed a sociable personality. He regarded these errands as a way of visiting with the folks who owned the frames. He left with the car in a spate of gravel from its tires and a blast backfiring from the exhaust.

When he returned, the Model-T Ford looked different. Sections of the quilting frame stuck out through open windows on both sides. The Ford took on the appearance of a prehistoric animal. I hid my laughter, knowing instinctively, that these were solemn moments.

Mama and Papa brought the quilting frame into our kitchen, where it covered the front door. It stood, looking out over the household activities, until the day the quilting began. Any secrets we may have had crept into its network of wood and tacks. Fastening the quilt-to-be on the frame was, in itself, an awesome task. First, it must be adjusted to the size of the quilt we wanted. Then the cloth had to be fastened to the frame by an ominous looking series of tacks that held their sharp end upwards. This was a laborious procedure.

Several times, Mama and Grandmother Julia removed the cloth from the tacks because the cloth did not appear to be straight enough or because the material was not taut enough. All work stopped then, until they felt satisfied that the material was fastened properly in the right position.

With a satisfied sigh, Mama decided the work was ready to go forward, and they began to "tie" the layers of cloth together. One layer was the backing - - often of dark blue percale - - the next layer was the woolen batting. They spread the rich mosaic of Mama's crazy quilt on top of that.

Mama and Grandmother, armed with vicious-looking needles, tied the quilt together, roughly six inches apart. This one was tied with pale blue yarn. As I watched, blue forget-me-nots with wings emerged. They captured my imagination, and I followed them through cloth gardens where paths were the seams sewed by the Singer sewing machine.

All day long, Mama and Grandmother sat there, stopping only for a cup of coffee and a piece of Mama's good bread covered with our own butter and jam. Sometimes, they talked, now and then lapsing into Norwegian. In this way, no doubt, they shared secrets, for the rest of us did not understand.

By late afternoon, the new quilt was birthed. Now, Mama would tuck in the raw edges and sew it together. I waited impatiently until it was off the frame so I could locate pieces of my blue skirt. Knowing the pieces were there seemed like having a secret. A wholesome storybook secret.

It seemed incredible to me that such ragged-edged pieces as Mama drew out of their hiding places could form a thing of beauty like that new quilt. And the whole thing happened because we saved the scraps.

§§§

twenty four

THE RADIO

On currents of the frost-encrusted air,
A wave of spirit richness met me there.

Outside the single window of our dining room, stars twinkled like tiny beacons frozen into place. A man's voice came over the airways to bring a wonder of words into our radio. That voice came from New York City, tripping in its channels high above Lake Erie and then sliding over Lake Michigan to its destination in our home.

The voice brought a wonderful new dimension to my life. I had furnished our small dairy farm with all the impossibilities an imagination can provide. I knew which cow in our herd had jumped over the moon.

I had sipped pretend tea with little people sitting around a mushroom that sprouted after a recent rain - - toadstool, we called it. I had thumbed a ride one afternoon with a goose that had slipped out of formation. Perched on its back, I went with it to the Big Rock Candy Mountain. To my disappointment, I could not break off chunks of candy.

I fiddled with the radio dial one night and came upon a golden nugget by chance. All the next week, I anguished over whether I should ask permission to listen to that hour of poetry the following week or if I should wait until everyone was asleep and sneak in to listen to the radio. I opted for asking permission and did so at mealtime, hoping that full stomachs would make everyone more agreeable. My question did not even provoke curiosity. Mama merely said "Just keep the sound low." The look she gave me was one of understanding.

On occasion, when static interfered, and our reception was nothing but a high-pitched squeal, I agonized over being unable to hear anything. I fiddled with the dial and held my breath. *Maybe. Just maybe some of his program would come through.* And, hopefully, I sat on the cold linoleum floor and waited. If I could hear even fifteen minutes of the production, the wait would be worth it. And, since then, I have learned more about that program presented over radio regularly. It originated in Kansas City where one day a station manager was in a tight spot. He had scheduled an hour of poetry, but the man who was going to read did not show up.

The manager pushed a book of poetry into the hands of a reporter named Alden Russell who happened to be at the station. "Here," the manager said, "You're going to read this for the next hour."

Alden was aghast. But he lacked a real reason to turn the manager down. He read the poetry, but drew the line with having his name associated with "that sissy stuff." At the close of the program he adlibbed "You have been listening to *Between the Bookends* by Ted Malone."

The program went well. It ran under that name for more than 25 years. The only lapse was when Russell went to Italy to work as a war correspondent.

As proof of its popularity, thousands of listeners wrote to Ted Malone with requests. Russell himself acquired a large library of poetry. Later, a volume of *Between the Bookends* was published annually.

"Hello there," Ted Malone began each time. And across the countryside listeners like myself feasted on his every word.

Life became transformed for me after the first time I heard *Between the Bookends.*

Yes, the times they were a-changing. And, in some respects, at least, for the better. Alden Russell had eased into an unaccustomed role in life. He began accumulating books of poetry and, in time, it became his own library. As for me, an exciting interest began the night I found Ted Malone on my radio dial in a farmhouse in a remote place in Minnesota. It has grown since then.

Those were hard times, we knew of drought, dropping prices on dairy products, and a glut of eggs and poultry on the market. We heard about a strike as near home as in St. Paul. To our shocked surprise, we read in our local paper about the conflict in Detroit. It was unbelievable that men armed with clubs and sticks fought with police carrying guns. We learned of this through radio broadcasts.

The magic of poetry delivered me from such concerns. For a while, nothing else mattered. I did not know it then, but the groundwork was laid for a love of poetry that would not diminish with the years. I came to realize, too, that it was free to others who looked for the same enjoyment - - It had no geographic or other boundaries.

While the members of my family slept, oblivious to what the radio could offer, I indulged in pleasure. I thrilled over the metric rhythm in poetry and savored the words chosen carefully to develop a thought or idea. I discovered insights into the language of the earth around me: bird calls, the rhythm of rain falling, the music of the river, the silent movement of the earth orbiting the sun, and magic of changing seasons.

As I sat captured by voices riding the airwaves, the flame of our kerosene lamp flickered. For the first time I noticed that its light created shadows on the papered walls of the dining room. I shifted from one side to another on the hard cold floor, alone, but not lonely.

My greatest misery was in the relentlessly passing minutes. The hour would be over. And then, I must wait for a week to hear that poetry again. I must bear the suspense of wondering if I would find the station in spite of airway interference.

Moonlight streamed through the windows, clear and bristling with cold. It traced the shadows of squared chair tops against the opposite wall. It seemed to be framed by the window casing. And, sometimes, to give an audio effect, I noticed that a piece of wood shifted with a splattering of sparks in the living room heating stove.

Across the decades, I carried with me the memory of that wonderful interlude that brought something unknown before and thoroughly delightful into my life. It is thrilling to me now to discover additional facts about the program.

Presented at many time slots, *Between The Bookends* took place from July of 1934 to September of 1938. The overall theme of Ted Malone's program was *Auld Lang Syne*.

The poetry I had read and memorized by Robert Louis Stevenson, Henry W. Longfellow and Sara Teasdale was like stepping stones to the poetry read by Ted Malone. I cried when the pathos was more than I could bear. I held nuggets of joy close to my heart. I remembered lines to take with me into the week, like bouquets of forget-me-nots that I found in the pasture when I went to drive the cattle home.

The radio in the dining room of our home brought the world to us in many different ways. In our innocence, we did not really understand what 'humor' was, but the radio brought what was publicly recognized as humor. If giggling over Fibber McGee and Molly was humor that was good enough for us. We had never been entertained in such a fashion before. We did not really understand, either, that the changing times were bringing measures of reform to people as forgotten as we were.

The radio introduced us to slang. It became popular to say "Whoopee!" for example, although we did not let Mama hear us say that. We might say, "Well, isn't that the cat's pajamas!" and then feel silly about using such an expression. We didn't know we were commenting on life by the use of slang.

With such means of communication, we learned about drought on a broader scale than ever before. We learned about social unrest and about military build-up in Europe. Overpowering worries like those made me grasp *Between The Bookends* with such eagerness. It was a release for me.

But, no discoveries ranked higher than the voice of Ted Malone. I heard its warmth when he read of the fears and longings of others. I heard his pain when he read about a victim of rejection. His voice reached into our rural isolation, broke down barriers, and drew me into the modern circle of humanity. The human voice accomplished what the impersonal voice of the press could not do.

He (Ted Malone) helped me to read with discrimination. I learned to reject coarse or rough language. Poetry that is written with sensitivity does not necessarily ignore the facts of living. It says something about them that transcends the ordinary. The poetry read by Ted Malone helped me to understand that we were part of a community. We had been isolated, a social entity by ourselves, but that would not continue. Changes were taking place. They would draw us into an unaccustomed position. Ted Malone's program offered much more than entertainment. It brought beauty into my home, besides introducing never-heard-before expressions.

The chilly floor of an unheated room became the springboard for enormous change. Change is born and reborn in an endless cycle. Sometimes, its birth pains overwhelm us. Sometimes, it evolves slowly, its presence too subtle for us to notice.

§§§

twenty five

THE CHRISTMAS CACTUS

Framed by a window looking south and east,
The cactus, blooming, was a visual feast.

The stand for the Christmas cactus was made of pine. Once, it had worn a coat of shiny varnish. But, a combination of sunlight that streamed through the south window, and water spilled over the edge of the saucer below the plant, had worn its varnish to a spotty finish.

While that might appear unfortunate, it also made the stand appropriate for its purpose. Nothing ought to detract from the beauty of the cactus that stood its ground throughout the four seasons.

The plant, as I remember it best, had prospered. It had grown segment by segment, until it escaped the pot in which it grew. In fact, it cascaded downward from the stand toward the floor.

My mother ministered to the cactus often, although it had only basic needs. It was a plant that seemed to draw interest, not entirely for its beauty but because of a magnetism it possessed. I felt sure it posed and preened for our benefit.

If any signs of pests appeared that endangered the cactus' life, my mother put in a telephone call to one of her sisters. "No," I heard her say, once, "I can't really see anything, but it seems droopy. It hasn't grown a bit for sometime now. If it could talk I think it would say it has a sore throat or something."

I noticed that my mother hovered over the plant for the next few days. She made a concoction of water and vinegar and a few drops of liniment (I think) and patted the leaves with a cloth soaked in the concoction. She hummed as she moved around the plant. The song she hummed was about a beautiful Indian maiden.

The cactus enjoyed many benefits. Enough, I believe, to keep any plant happy. From their enlarged photos hanging on the wall, Grandfather Olaf and Grandmother Anna stared at the plant as if to memorize every detail of its appearance.

And, when we had our sing-a-longs in the evening, we clustered around the organ a few feet away from the plant stand. One after another we sang those hymns to the same God who piloted the grandparents away from their native Sweden. One after another we sang along with the rich chords of the organ that had only two or three discordant keys.

There was just one instance of trauma that would have affected the plant. One night, our papa rose from his bed to attend a personal chore. The moon shone brightly through the windows, and he saw no need to light a lamp.

Suddenly, a horrific noise and clatter awakened us from our sleep. Papa had walked into a mousetrap and wore it on his big toe. In his fright and pain, he lunged into the plant stand, knocking it over on the organ.

One by one, we awakened and visited the scene of the accident. We knew without being told, that making sure of Papa's welfare was our first concern. Then, we picked up the cactus that had slipped down to the floor and set it back on the stand.

The damage was surprisingly little. A few leaves, a few blossoms and a slight tilt to its posture summed it up.

The damage to Papa's dignity was considerable. We rained attention on him for a few days which he liked so much we had a hard time pulling away.

The cactus was not always in bloom. Its drooping, pink, bell-like blossoms disappeared periodically when the plant was dormant. For a few weeks then, it stood naked and waiting.

My mother gave it the same care as ever. Tirelessly, she worked the soil with a table fork to keep it aerated. With regularity she fed it plant food. And, with equal regularity, she fed it the dregs of her coffee cup (laced generously with cream and sugar).

It took note when soft winds of spring unlocked the land, and water trickled in make-believe rivers along the shrinking drifts of snow. It observed the first thunderstorm of the season and cringed at the booming blasts of thunder. It waited tremendously for the first timid mayflowers to bloom near the roots of the honeysuckle bushes just beyond the window.

And, at the same time, the cactus sighed with patience rewarded. For now, it had company outside. It stretched its cactus leaves luxuriously.

It stood there when Grandmother Anna died. It shuddered when her body was taken away. Grandmother Anna had spoken to it when there was no one else around. Now, it would hear no more Swedish endearments.

The cactus prospered. It received the succor it needed. Its ears thrived on the music we provided. My mother met its needs to be touched as she applied moisture to its leaves with soft cloths. It had room enough to stretch out and flex its muscles to prevent growing pains.

I think it joined us in our prayers. While they were a private matter, they were no less devout. Their spiritual thrust must have enriched the life of the cactus.

When visitors were ushered into the room to see the plant in bloom, we all shared the pride. The cactus was like one of the family. It seemed animate to us.

Most likely, it shared our grief after our mother was no longer living.

That chapter of life had ended. Yet it is not completely gone. If I close my eyes and blink, I can open them to see a vision of the cactus brimful of life. Its blossoms tumble downward from the simple pine stand.

It has a kind of eternal life, because memory of it is so powerful. While that one Christmas cactus was a part of our family life, there are others like it. They bloom and gladden the hearts of those who admire them.

§§§

twenty six

THE ROOM

A host of memories stretch and loiter there,
And rock the years away in that old chair.

I can go there anytime I want to. That room is so firmly fixed in my mind that I can get there in seconds. You might place is a retreat. The remotes and push-button features of electronic instruments transport us to another world. But nothing there matches the charms of a room that will live forever to me.

That room has changed now, for the house has been remodeled. Whatever its present condition, it does not really matter. The place remains, the same to me. While some photographs exist, I prefer the picture that stays firmly in my mind.

When the room was available to me to visit, I could never decide how I liked it best. Sometimes, I thought it was when the sun was overhead. Then the room was shady and placid-looking. Rich crimson threads in the braided rugs (brought out their brightness like fugitives waiting their moment of release).

Once I believed no other place would bring me such peace as that room. I was wrong. If I bring with me a believing and patient heart, it is possible to find scarlet threads in the warp and woof of other places. That brightness does not go unrivaled.

I do not suppose I can give you a single reason why that room was so dear to me. I loved the people who came to the room, but that was not the only reason. Neither is that fondness kept only for happenings that took place in the room. Not too long ago, I saw other places with bay windows, like those in my favorite room. The windows, in themselves, stirred nothing but a lukewarm kind of admiration.

It is not true, either, that all my experiences in that room were happy ones. Friends, relatives and neighbors came there - - not always happy to be together. Even stirring up those old coals of bitterness and hostility, however, does not undermine the tug of strong feeling I have for that room.

On a winter afternoon, the scene from the bay window is framed forever in my heart. A sweep of snowy acres from which cold sunlight captured rhinestone reflections dazzles me as I think about it.

As the sun swept westward to its descent beyond view, small dips in the drifted snow filled up with lavender shadows. The colorful show continued until the sun went on to its westward mission. And, then, gray shadows engulfed the land until even the dull crimson line where sky met land was overcome.

That room of which I am still fond gave me its own individual view of what I found to be breathtaking beauty. Some of the beauty was outside, but much of it was inside. Even shabby pieces of furniture were good looking in that surrounding cleanliness. The gilt curlicues of the huge frames of our family pictures gave proof of their beauty. Ruffled pads of the wooden rocker dared anyone to get them dirty.

112

Within that room, I heard unique noises. The creaking of rocking chairs, quiet footfalls on a braided rug, or a hush, sometimes, that seemed to be full of voices no longer heard there.

I knew the room did not offer luxury, but it offered comfort. It taught me the difference. I learned there that some things go together and some do not. I'm not speaking only of things, but of people too. And sounds and words.

I loved that room I knew so well. I knew the places in the floor that might creak if you wanted them not to. That room was probably my favorite of all time although I have favorites now, too.

That favorite room had a kind of a heartbeat. It gave you a welcome if you stopped to know it. It wept tears of moisture on the leaves of the Christmas cactus that bloomed on the library table for a long time. It sighed a voice that could be furnace hummings, but which I believe was its own way of speaking.

I believe the depth of my prayers were born in that room. They breathed from a full heart whose thanks brim over to this day. They groaned with hurts and fears. They pumped something generous and all-suffering into my bloodstream that gushes for evermore.

That room was a kind of a refuge. Still it was sometimes over-run with people. Even your most sacred moments were in danger of being invaded.

If I had to choose which object in that room was my favorite, I would select the wooden rocker. If I were to choose any favorite feature, it would be the bay window always covered with lace panels. It seemed like a kind of a sanctuary.

The window made a frame for all I could see of God's earth. It taught me a lesson. Even if that bay window had framed a vista of extraordinary beauty, I could not love it more.

I believe that God gives us as much to look at as we can take in.

§§§

twenty seven

THE HEATING STOVE

My fingers on the firebox could feel,
Its ice cold trim above a field of steel.

Mama and Papa took the stove pipes down one day. When I came home from school I found them hard at work putting the heating stove in storage for the summer months. Its nickel plated fenders where we toasted our toes on severely cold days had been stripped away and put into storage.

When I opened the stove door I saw nothing but grates that were empty and useless. Maybe I just imagined having seen the firebox stoked with fuel. Maybe it was just a dream that flames crept on scarlet feet along the chunks of wood placed there. Maybe it was a fantasy that the belly of the big heater fairly trembled with its burning cargo that sent funnels of smoke through the stove- pipes and out the chimney. Although the sun was on summer schedule through longer, warmer days, it somehow failed to compensate for that dismantled heating stove. I imagined it folded its cold arms around its bulging body, comforting itself for not being able to provide heat even on rainy, windy days. I imagined that it trembled until its lids clattered with regret for having its heating job taken away from it.

I imagined that it shook with grief over being exiled to a hallway where no one could pull up a chair and move closer. I imagined its tears, all in vain, over being put into a corner for several months until its heating skills were needed again.

Its cumbersome body was covered by an old quilt no longer considered good enough to cover a bed. When I came near, I pulled it closer around the body of the heater and then giggled to realize that I was trying to cover up the stove whose job it was to throw out heat.

If we had visitors, we sat in the living room as usual. But, the place where the heater stood during winter month became a naked, yawning place. It seemed to me it looked around as if wondering what to do now with the heater gone.

Even the mourning doves that put in an appearance sometime in June could not appease my grief over the dismantled front room heater. Eating fresh peas from the garden by the handfuls should have compensated, but it did not. Having fresh strawberries in cream for breakfast did not even make up the loss.

Washing my hair in rainwater caught in the big barrel below the down-spouting that drained from the roof came close to compensating. And, yet, even then I threw longing looks at the heater under its shroud huddling in the hallway by the stairs.

"It won't be long before you're in the living room again," I whispered to the heater. That was actually a lie, partly because I did not know when Mama and Papa would return the heater to its rightful place in the living room.

Even worse, I had overheard Mama and Papa talking about the heater. They were interested in another model, for they contemplated changing their fuel from wood, which was running out, to coal. I shuddered, for having to get used to a different living room stove seemed more than I could bear. When I walked past the heater on my way upstairs, I looked at it in a forlorn way.

Summer went by in a succession of dry spells and rainy spells. To use Papa's words, "summer went by on greased skids." I had no idea what greased skids were, for they were not a part of my vocabulary.

It's true, the summer days raced quickly enough. We had canned all the peas and beans. Tomatoes, too. We had preserved many bushels of apples given to us by someone in the neighborhood who had what he called "a bumper crop."

We bought what Mama called "lugs" of peaches and pears from storekeepers in Mora. And, yes, lugs of what Papa called "Eye-talian" plums. While I liked the sauce Mama made from those plums, I disliked the foreign feeling of that fruit. The apple sauce Mama made, with the pulp of the apple softening to a shapeless, mashed consistency was my idea of a real sauce. Yes, it was "Jim-dandy" as I heard Papa say.

So, the summer season passed in a series of long, hot days and nights whose hours were torn by storms that produced thunder and lightening and too infrequently, pelting showers. Whenever I passed the heating stove in the front hall closet, I felt pain to see it so useless. I felt sure that it must have found the summer almost endless, standing in the hallway not seeing anyone except those bound for upstairs.

I was in school the day Mama and Papa returned the heating stove to its place in the living room. I rejoiced when I saw that it sported a shiny elbow of pipe Papa said would make it "draw" better. While I had no idea how a stove could draw, the term satisfied me.

When the days grew shorter, and the north wind had a decided whine, it felt satisfying to pull up close to the heater in the living room again. I found reassurance because the stove returned to the living room. Once more, mittens lined up, steaming on the nickel-plated fenders. Once more, we stood as close as possible in order to soak up some of the warmth before going up the cold stairs to a bedroom heated only by warmth creeping through a register on the floor.

We did not benefit much from the efforts of that heating stove in our bedroom on second floor, but the fact that it was there pumping out all the warmth it could manage was a distinct comfort.

The heating stove had a prominent role in our lives. It always seemed more animate to me than a mere fixture dispensing heat.

§§§

twenty eight
THE LAMPS

When, rosy-heeled, the sun moved out of sight,
Our lamps provided us with pools of light.

After the sun slipped out of the sky through a bank of clouds, the last light shone on the neighbor's vast field to the west. The sun, it seemed to me, belonged to that neighbor. I believed that he held its light as long as possible so that he could finish more of his duties. No doubt, I had learned in school that the earth revolves around the sun but felt more inclined to depend on what appeared to be true.

Then, we lit the lamps and lanterns. Their wicks and mantles would provide us with light until dawn of another day. Their feeble light fell short of being satisfactory, but since we had nothing with which to compare, we felt satisfied.

And, it follows, that anything used every day must undergo cleaning at some time or other.

Like other kids of twelve years, I could hardly wait to be considered grown up enough to do any job. If a job was off limits, it seemed desirable. One day, I learned that I had advanced to become a part of the crew that washed lamps and lanterns.

The first step consisted of going to the various rooms to pick up the lamps from each location and bring them to the kitchen. The lanterns hung in a row on nails in the back porch. I saved them for last. I started with the lamps upstairs, proceeding downward with the greatest care.

Unable to resist an opportunity to fantasize, I talked to the lamps in the kitchen. "I won't drop you, I promise. You're going to feel a lot better when that smoked up chimney is clean. This won't take long. Soon you'll be back in your usual place."

Having bumped up against the utter reality in the minds of most grown-ups before, I prudently kept my voice to a whisper. This must be between myself and the lamps. I felt sure we would get along well.

When the lamps were placed on the kitchen table, and their chimneys set aside, they looked forlorn. They were like Mama's chickens that had to be separated at times - - the hens from the roosters.

After the separation, they looked forlorn and droopy. Even the roosters did not seem cock-sure.

Soon, I was kept too busy to think anymore about the condition of the lamps or their chimneys. When they had been washed in hot suds, I rinsed them and wiped them dry. Seeing the chimneys sparkle gave me a reward for my labors.

This particular job gave me a different look at the towels. All of them were made from flour sacks, hemmed and often embroidered on the corners. The newer ones were stiff for some time. I learned to use them on the covers of pots and pans.

But, the job of cleaning the lamps taught me that for this work I must use the older, softer towels. I had to push a towel inside a lamp chimney and twist it around to wipe the glass until it shone. I had never suspected that towels were anything but square, hemmed pieces of cloth. Now, I knew they had different purposes at different stages of wear. I would remember that when we folded them after completion of the laundry.

Mama did not talk much as she worked, she hummed. Sometimes she hummed familiar hymns. Not much could be wrong with our lives when our Mama hummed at her work.

While the lamp operation appeared to be simply washing the lamps and the globes, it included giving the wicks attention, and filling the lamps with fuel. We had a supply of wicks we had bought by the yard. They had to be cut into proper lengths for the size of the lamp.

We threaded the wicks through the burner of the lamp. The bottom part of the wick lay in kerosene in the body of the lamp. When it was saturated, a lighted match ignited the wick.

After a wick had been used for some time, the top part became charred. Then, the wick burned irregularly, and caused a flickering light. The uneven wicks smoked up lamp chimneys. To avoid that, the wicks had to be trimmed before they could be used again.

That job, needless to say, required some judgment and expertise. I did not graduate to that level of performance until I was old enough to do almost anything. By that time, the job had lost its glamour for me.

After the lamps received their needed attention, they were returned to their places. That was my part of the job. I relished the chance because it gave me additional opportunity to dramatize my role.

"Now, don't you feel a lot better?" I asked the tall-chimneyed lamp that stood on a library table in the living room. I looked around the room. All was in order.

Every lamp became a personality to me, the short, squatty one that wished it were taller. The tallest one needed to sparkle the most because it stood head and shoulders above the rest. The one with a burner that we could never polish clean - - "It's okay," I reassured it. "We only look at the flame anyway."

On the days we cleaned the lamps, I ignored the table on which the Coleman lamp stood. Lighting it was an elaborate procedure that only our Papa controlled. Papa pumped air into the body of the lamp. And, when he set a match to the mantle, it leaped into flame with a gasp - - we gasped with it as though it was required of us.

I realized without being told that the Coleman lamp was not on our cleaning list. It existed in a class by itself.

The lanterns, too, were treated differently. Their mantles, of a different nature, required only the touch of a match to light them.

At times, when Papa lighted a lantern and went out to the barn to finish his work, I watched as he walked across the yard. The unlighted blackness was frightening to me. Sometimes, the wind blew hard against the lantern. The flame flickered and then appeared to be close to snuffing out.

I feared for Papa then, sure that the darkness would devour him. Not until I saw the lantern light burning from the barn did I relax. The lantern seemed so small a thing against a world of darkness.

Lanterns needed to be washed, too. Kerosene emptied into a funnel placed in a small opening in the tank, accumulated in a greasy film around the lantern tank. That must be washed periodically.

The globe was enclosed in a framework of heavy metal. We seldom took that out. Instead, we washed the entire lantern. When the film of grease and grime were removed, the lantern looked like a dirty-faced child who was given the soapy wash-cloth treatment.

The lamps and lanterns were vital to our welfare. I liken them now to the lives of people who have a purpose. Like wicks, they burn steadily, sometimes worn down but always casting light in dark places.

§§§

twenty nine

THE NEWSPAPERS

Stacks of papers strewn across the floor - -
How could a reading family ask for more?

A neighbor who lived south and east of our farm subscribed to the daily newspaper as well as the Sunday paper. We were in awe of such obvious wealth.

Periodically, the tall thin, pleasant man made visits to our farm. During winter months he pulled a child's sled full of newspapers accumulated at their house. In summer, he did the same thing, but used a child's wagon.

The fact that the papers were out-dated did not matter to us. We savored every one of them. They offered diversion from tiresome routine. And, they brought news from the outside world. Because they were bigger than the Kanabec County Times (a weekly newspaper), we considered them to be much more desirable.

Exciting though those papers were when they arrived, I had to ask permission before I could start reading them. That luxury was a conditional matter. My homework for school must have top priority - - even arithmetic which I hated. And, I must not quarrel with my siblings over the choice of reading matter.

It was hard to keep from quarreling when a sibling dawdled over material I wanted to read.

Sometimes, we passed the papers on to another family of readers. We kept them in good condition, except for removing bits here and there. Although those bits were clipped out neatly, the paper was never the same again.

News pieces furnished us with fresh input for reports in school. The advice to lovelorn columns brought dramatic situations that we could drool over. They made our life seem stodgy by comparison.

Pieces that covered the "industrial revolution" were choice bits. That revolution seemed a long way from our farm, but we knew it was true because the newspaper writers had said so. If, sometimes, I didn't believe those opinions wholeheartedly, I did not say so out loud. I felt awe for those writers whose names appeared in print.

Sometimes, I put my name up there by one of the articles to see how it would look. That was a pretend game that I never told anyone about. If I had someone would have told me, "Don't be so forward!"

While Mama's time was more restricted, she liked the papers, too. She looked for recipes that she might want to clip. When she did, those recipes were added to a pile in one of the sewing machine drawers. To my knowledge, they were never used.

Sometimes, Mama cut out dress patterns. They, too, had a drawer in the sewing machine cabinet. Once in a while, Mama would paste some coins to a piece of cardboard and mail them to an address given. We gathered around excitedly when those patterns came in the mail. The mailman didn't stop at our mailbox too often; it was a grand occasion when he did.

The comic strips offered us material for thought and conversation. "Bringing Up Father" was a favorite. Sometimes, at the supper table we talked about Jiggs and his love for corned beef and cabbage. And, we were united in our disgust with Maggie who wanted to crash the upper social circles where corned beef and cabbage were considered a vulgar kind of food.

We laughed privately or with each other over the absurdity of Li'l Abner, Mammy and Pappy Yoakum, and Daisy Mae.

The characters of those strips became like real life people. In fact, during my illness with scarlet fever, I had a recurring dream. A woman whom I had dubbed Mrs. Andy Gump walked through those dreams. When the high temperatures raged, that woman was real to me. She walked around carrying a little red purse high ahead of her. I wanted that little red purse so I followed dream-lady. I caused Mama and Papa endless concern, for they were sure I would follow her, sleep-walking out into the cold.

Blondie, forever teetering around in her high-heeled shoes seemed like the girl next door. Later, I made the discovery that our Blondie had ventured far out into the world. A comic strip in Buenos Aires brought that same Blondie to their reading public.

My hungry eyes searched for the romance novel serialized in the newspaper. If we were first in the line of readers, we had to leave the novel there for the next readers. If the newspapers came from other friends and neighbors, we might be last.

In that case, we clipped out the installment, and it became one of the others issued. Then, we were privileged to cut out that portion of the novel and keep it. We put them together with a safety pin and saved them for future re-reads.

On a few occasions, we read the newspapers and clipped out pieces to our hearts' content. We did not know they were going on to other readers. By the time it reached those other readers, the paper looked very much like a house whose windows and doors stood wide open.

Whatever was going on in our lives - - heartaches or headaches - - they became more tolerable when we had a fresh stack of newspapers to devour.

§§§

thirty

THE EXTRAVAGANZA

They flashed around us every summer night,
Those glow-worms, tracing patterns in their flight.

I held my breath - - first one, then two, then more that I could count. They came to life out of the darkness. They were glow-worms, which we sometimes called fireflies.

When my reading brought me to an explanation of how glow-worms function, I was both sad and glad. Glad to know what makes them glow, and sad to lose my sense of wonderment.

Glow-worms were important, because they offered interest to us. In the country, I had no access to recreational parks. No ferris-wheels, thrill rides or even a merry-go-round. We wouldn't be able to get to them unless they were accessible in some place like Mora.

But, I was not deprived. I had a wonderful backyard, so familiar to me that I could walk around blindfolded. I knew every tree and every bush. I knew the paths that went to the other areas of the yard, and I knew the big willows where our swing dawdled, unless it had a rider.

It was here the drama began on summer evenings. Our yard was heavy with foliage. Deep pools of darkness lay under the wide branches of pine and spruce trees. A line of lilac bushes held their heavily-leafed, tangly twigs massed together like a curtain. The big willow tree draped long boughs over black pits of mystery.

By daylight, the yard was divided into sections, such as the front yard, the back yard, and the garden side, but in the darkness those dividers were invisible unless the moon shone brightly on a well-trodden path.

We made a game of watching the fireflies. How many winked from the tallest spruce? How many lit their lanterns among the grasses snug to the ground? We made up silly reasons why some stayed in the grass - - Maybe some got dizzy if they stayed up high. Maybe they listened for messages that were transmitted through the earth. Maybe they were divided into Higher-Up Troops and Close-to-the-ground Troops. We were always going to stay up all night to see if they ever went to bed - - but we never did.

I told no one else about my private term for the fireflies - - I called them "lanterns of adventure." It made me feel good to have that name for those winged creatures.

Although we were fascinated by the fireflies, we did not ignore other sensations. Standing beside the pine trees, I smelled the musty odor of the duff that lay below the trees. I strummed my fingers over the feathery branches of the willow and the prickly needles of the pine.

We didn't simply *watch* the fireflies - - we experienced them. They were a dependable part of the night world - - like stars and the Northern Lights.

The dream world in which I often lived opened its door wider. I found the light in both stars and glow worms a kind of miracle, regardless of the reasons behind them.

I did not understand what makes them glow. I did not know until much later that oxygen, breathed through the creature's organs, combines with another substance. Nerves in the insect's light-making organ control the timing of the flashes. While that information robbed me of the sense of mystery about them, it satisfied me too. God had put them together in such a fashion to make us more aware of them.

Experts tell us that the male gives us the first wink of light. In the most common North American firefly, the male flies around and flashes every five seconds. The female stays on the ground and responds about two seconds later.

But, as watchers, we were caught up in the display itself. When darkness fell on our farm on a summer evening, our grassy, leafy world seemed full of wondering silence. Twilight deepened, and the last strip of rosy color in the west dimmed to nothingness. Birdsongs became hushed.

A time of waiting. I often felt suspended between day's end and the new day's beginning. I tried to think of something similar to those flashing lights. *They were like tiny candles piercing a small pool of darkness. And, yes, they were like suddenly understanding something that had been cocooned in Ignorance for a long time.*

§§§

thirty one

THE GRANARY

Dust motes danced along in beams of light,
That streamed through every spider web in sight.

Outside, the shingled roof of the granary came down to the edge like a big upper lip. All along that edge, barn swallows had built their mud-wattled nests. At evening, you could hear the cheep-cheeping and you could see them swooping down over the meadows to feed on mosquitoes or gnats which they caught "on the fly".

Inside, dust motes danced through the light filtering down from the windows high up above. I liked the granary. I examined a new spider web near the door to admire its intricate structure. When it shook from a draft let in through the door, I held my breath.

And, I drew in the odors of the granary. They were a big part of my fascination with the building. There was nothing like it anywhere; a composite of dried plants that rode on the wings of the four winds, together with the crumbling petals of matured flowers. The dried hulls of grain gone to seed.

Back in the house helping Mama in the kitchen, I had mixed feelings when Mama said (as she often did) "Go and get some ground grain for me, please." We fed the ground grain to the chickens in the form of mash, poured into a large wooden trough.

While liking the granary, I hated that chore because of the big, red-wattled rooster that pushed in and hurried the hens out. Mama told me to make him go away, but his self-important bustling scared me - - And, sometimes he pecked at my legs.

Two wooden steps led up to the granary. Their unpainted wood had weathered to a nothing color. They were not pretty to look at, but I liked the fact that feet had worn the steps thinner in the middle. Sometimes, I stopped and fit my feet into the grooves of countless feet before me.

Although the granary was not a big building, it seemed large to me because it had a high-pitched roof. The small windows near the peak threw sunlight across the roomy space overhead - - producing an airy feeling.

Some of the spider webs fastened to the beams looked like bits of lacy curtain. They stirred in breezes that blew through the open door. Papa swept them down when he had time, but soon there were new ones.

I didn't leave the granary as soon as I had poured out the ground grain for Mama's chickens. It was more fun to dawdle for a while. Sometimes, I stopped by the oats bin and ran my fingers through those hard grain kernels. If I listened closely to the whispering noises they made while sifting through my fingers, I might understand what they said.

Our granary was separated into bins. And, they were made of unpainted boards that ran diagonally from the roughly cut beams to the floor. They fitted closely to the beams and the floor so that the grain could not spill out of any cracks.

Sacks filled with ground grain stood against a wall. They sagged together, looking like fat ladies with double chins, waiting for a ride. I started to talk to them one day, but Papa came around the corner and I turned off the conversation until later.

Rough boards covered the floor. Although the wood had never been painted, it had been swept clean often enough to acquire a soft sheen.

After ground grain had been emptied out of the gunny sacks, they were folded and stacked on the floor in the corner. Once, somebody left sacks draped over the sides of bins. Papa was upset when he found them. For a long time he scolded about the infringement of an unspoken rule.

I asked Papa, after our trip to the grain mill, why the place was so messy. Papa said that the men working there did not have time to pick up after every grinding operation. But, I saw Papa through different eyes afterward, and our clean, tidy, granary made me feel proud.

The process of planting grain, watching for signs of pests, such as thistle, and then harvesting it, remained a mystery for a long time. Once, though, I heard Papa say that our oats harvested "twenty bushels to the acre," and it was worth only $2.50 a bushel.

Strangely enough, it was learning about the "twenty bushels to the acre" and worth $2.50 a bushel that impressed me most. This was like reading a story and finding out the characters are real people. I suddenly saw a purpose to the tilling, and the seeding, and the harvesting. Our welfare was directly related to the price paid for our products, including grain.

While I did not understand the mysteries of the big grain market in Minneapolis, harvest and grain prices were the pieces that fit each other. Even our granary. There, we stored the grain for our use and the grain we sold to the Co-Op. I thought of the plump sacks standing by the walls, and I thought of the creamy colored oats waiting in the bins.

It was time to bring the grain to Mama for the chickens. I carefully latched the door, taking one last look upward to where the light filtered through a crack in the wall. "How I wish!" I said, in a whisper, "I could stay here longer!"

Air sighed through the closing door, it promised to say more if I listened. I promised to come back soon.

Our granary had a lot to tell.

§§§

thirty two
THE SPOKESMAN

Before the morning's light, his clarion call
Had pierced the deepest dreams of one and all.

The chicken coop, a small building, appeared to have sprouted on its site and grown up there. The surface of one wall sported a tarpaper covering, while an adjacent wall had a finish of siding. Its shape was irregular, and it had a dashing air of not minding its strange appearance at all.

Inside, the coop held long rows of nests which Papa had built. The long troughs in the chicken yard during summer months resided inside the coop during winter. During those months, the floor became hard to navigate since little space remained clear.

Although the barn stood some distance away, chickens moved freely in between it and the chicken coop. Chickens tended to be quite conversational, and I thought their dividing time between barn and coop was a good sociable arrangement.

We fed the chickens a mash made of ground grain and water. I found this a disagreeable chore since it included rinsing an accumulation of droppings from the troughs.

In addition to the mash, we threw whole grain into the chicken yard or coop floor morning and evening. Beside that, Mama came from the kitchen at regular intervals to toss handfuls of bread crumbs toasted too brown for human consumption, pieces of pancake left on plates, bits of fried pork rind and raisins culled out by those who didn't consider raisins edible.

Those same delicacies attracted crows that came flying noisily in for a feast. They must have laughed at Mama who yelled, "Get away! Shoo! Shoo!" and shook her apron in a threatening gesture. Mama couldn't look fierce if she tried!

The crows moved in anyway and made off with as much as they could gobble down. Their loud calls drifted behind them as they departed.

A log beam capped the roof of the chicken house. Pigeons congregated there to add soft comments. Papa tried to scare them away, but I thought we should leave them alone. I felt sure that Noah included pigeons in his ark, and that gave them some sacred purpose.

Out of that chicken compound, one of Mama's laying hens strolled on a spring day and headed for the barn. During the last couple of days, she had begun acting secretive and cranky, the typical signs of a brooding hen.

I understood. She wanted to build a nest, fill it with eggs and assume the role of mother to a bunch of chicks.

She headed toward a sheltered corner of the barn, out of sight and secluded. There she could escape attention. The cows were not apt to bother her, nor any other creature.

Mama objected to the hen's determination. "I need those eggs." she stormed. "Most likely a skunk or a weasel will get them before they hatch anyway."

But in this case Mama was mistaken. One day, sometime later, the brood hen came strutting out of the barn. She fluffed her feathers as if adding bulk would add to her dignity. She walked with a majestic air, triumph written in every line of her body. The chicks following were her accomplishment. They hustled to keep up with their mother. A couple of them, weaker than the others, dragged one wing behind.

Mother hen, her matronly pride full blown but still swelling, back-tracked to the rear, prodded the two hang-behinders, and continued on around the hen house with her brood.

As I followed the brood hen and her flock between the coop and the barn, I thought often of echoes of the bell from the church that Grandfather Olaf helped build. I felt sure they waited, hidden in corners and behind doors, to emerge again.

Since the chicks had become a reality in the farm yard, Mama chose to take a maternal view of the matter. In a few weeks they would be grown and would add to her poultry wealth. "Don't let them get out in the tall grass," she warned, "They might get killed."

One day, as I watched, a large garter snake coiled itself nearby and prepared to strike at a little chick. The stick in my hand became a weapon, and I struck savagely at the reptile. Mother hen, scolding noisily, gathered her flock and led them into the chicken yard, for it seemed to represent safety .

As the chicks grew bigger, we had front row seats for watching their progress. They sprouted wattles and combs that developed with the passing days. The roosters became roosters noticeably.

One of them, wandering around without any particular purpose, suddenly spied another rooster whose conduct annoyed him. Charging from across the chicken yard, he flew at the offender. Feathers fluttered about in the fracas. Hens scattered, uttering cries of protest that seemed too weak to be of any use.

The one self-designated as winner strutted importantly around, poking at the ground for no apparent reason. He crowed, too, a funny, scratchy cock-a-doodle-doo that hardly seemed like a cry of victory. Ruffling his feathers, he stalked from one end of the chicken yard to the other, rehearsing and practicing his "cock-of-the-walk" stride.

When the same rooster charged into a gathering of hens for no apparent reason, I cautioned him. "You better watch out. Mama is going to butcher chickens soon. If she sees how you're acting, you'll be the first to go!"

Mama sent me to the coop frequently to check on the chickens before closing it up for the night. IT was my job to see that they were all on the roosts. If a skunk or a weasel (or even a fox) found its way into the coop, the chickens highest up on the roosts were the safest.

In the midst of such a scene, a weasel crept into the henhouse one night. The clatter of frightened poultry and the uproar of disoriented chickens reached us where we slept in our beds and demanded action. Mama issued an "everybody-out-of-bed" call to the household. We responded with sleepy protests, all the while shrugging on sweaters and jackets. Seconds later, we reached the coop.

"He got away with one," Mama lamented, almost instantly. Sure enough, a trail of blood and feathers made plain to us the route the robber had taken when he left. "The door was locked," Mama continued "So, he got in through a hole somewhere." That silenced a worry I had felt. I had done my job well enough, but the hen that was taken was no doubt sleeping near the floor of the henhouse.

No one commented on Mama's assumption that the intruder was of the male and usually more aggressive gender. It seemed to be a safe assumption, and Papa did not object out loud, at least.

We set about quieting the chickens, assuring them with soothing voices that they would be all right now. Gradually, they settled in again with only an occasional squawk from one of the hens with a longer memory than the rest.

Then, one of them let out a cry full of fear. And I would once more take on the lullaby responsibility until the creature quieted down. When they were sleeping on their roosts, clucking softly to themselves, we crept quietly out of the door and went back to our beds, hoping to get warm under the covers.

For a few days following the break-in, Mama vented her dismay over the loss of a good chicken and a reduction in egg count. "I'm going to set traps," she announced.

We knew she wouldn't, partly because there was too much work for her to handle already. Partly because we felt sure the extra safety measures taken to strengthen the foundation of the coop would make traps unnecessary.

Little by little, we restored order to the poultry area. We fed the chickens, cleaned up their coop and their feeding troughs, tidied up their roosts, and added fresh straw to the nests.

When one of the young roosters issued a cock-a-doodle-doo call from a funny, hoarse throat, we laughed heartily. It was good to laugh and put the chicken tragedy behind us.

We were relieved too, that Papa had reinforced the outside support to the coop. Mama would be lost without her egg money - - and so, as a matter of fact, would we.

Our poultry count did not stop at chickens either. A pair of turkeys claimed a portion of the yard as theirs. You might say they took over the guarding duty from the dog. Having no time for strangers, they ran folks off the yard unless stopped.

The pair of them, pretty as a picture - - to use the term loosely - - poked around the yard, the chicken coop and the barn. When they were near, I walked with a stout stick in my hand. A rather foolish precaution since I took to my heels at the very sight of them, leaving little dust clouds that followed my racing feet.

Pap wasn't satisfied with the addition of two turkeys, for he added a goose and a gander. I thought they were a nuisance, because, territorial by nature, they considered a portion of our yard as their private estate.

Since the boundaries of that piece of real estate were of uncertain dimensions, it left me feeling uneasy.

That's not all, the goose and gander took a liking to my hide-away under the poplar trees. I did not like sharing that space. The droppings from geese were numerous, too, and that made my hide-away dirty and uninviting.

The gander was hard to get along with. He roamed around like a feathered detective with his long neck outstretched. He appeared ready to attack.

Often, Papa led him around with a hand on his long neck. After accompanying Papa around the yard for a while, gander's disposition took a decided turn for the worse. He had a taste of feeling important.

The hissing became more menacing, and he seemed out of control. That was, in fact, his undoing. One day after doing tour duty with Papa, he spied my little sister running across the yard. He beat his wings with a noise that sounded like war drums, revved up his speed and took off after her.

Papa must have been scared. He picked up the first thing he found which happened to be an ax and flung it at the gander. His aim was accurate. The gander had taken its final tour.

He was last seen on a platter beside his mate where they supplied our dinner. The turkeys weren't exactly popular either. Shortly afterward, they too supplied the meat for our dinner.

As for the poultry, they were harmless, with one exception. These bland, usually gentle-natured chickens that tucked their heads beneath their wings at night and cooed sweetly in their sleep, were capable of savagery, too. If one of their number became scratched so a speck of blood showed on some part of its anatomy, the others gathered like so many red combed or wattled warriors and moved in for the kill.

Their daily pursuits of scratching in the yard, and harmless searches in the garden became submerged by an urge to kill. They pecked at the poor, innocent chicken, that had unwittingly become injured, until it was close to death. They would have gone on if we had not mercifully taken it away to heal in some safer location.

The funniest scene in the chicken yard of my recollection was the day two roosters found the same angleworm. Each one claimed its legal rights, and they played tug-of-war. There was not much left of the earth-colored creature by the time they began tasting their treat.

However many changes took place in the poultry area, I never tired of gathering the eggs, feeling the warm shells that were strong and yet so delicate. While I resented the crankiness of the hens that pecked at my hand when I claimed their produce, I could not actually blame them for not liking to part with the eggs. They were all the hens had to show for their occupation.

Owners of large poultry produce farms never get to know their chickens as we knew ours. Never will they understand our concern when one of them had a lifeless comb that would not stay upright. Never will they feel the pride we felt in cleaning and polishing the eggs until they shone so we would get top pay.

With pride we brought our small egg case into Mora. We never let on that the small check we got in return hardly made it worthwhile.

Owners of large produce farms will never feel the pride we felt when Sir Rooster crowed at 4:25 a.m. Proudly and snobbishly, as we had seen him parading around the chicken yard or coop, he stood on his roost and issued his morning call.

He knew he was prompt with his awakening act. He knew it carried into our bedrooms where we plumped our pillows and stretched and sometimes bargained for a few more minutes of sleep.

Sir Rooster still struts through the halls of my best memories.

§§§

thirty three

THE LILACS

I was surprised again year after year,
To see the fragrant blossoms reappear.

Three of them. Nothing unusual about three lilac bushes except that they were planted in the middle of our field. Because there were three and because of their location, they aroused interest. Throughout my years of living, they had been a legend.

"Who put them there?" "Why are they there?" "Did they mark some sort of sacred spot?" "How long have they been there?"

It would seem these bushes had been planted near the close of the nineteenth century. Most likely they were sprouts from lilac bushes in our yard. Someone dug them up with care.

Transplanting is a simple enough act, but bushes would need nurture if they were to grow to maturity. They would have needed fertilizer and water. They would have needed to be kept free of weeds which, by tradition, grow strong and rapidly.

One thing is certain, they could not have grown to maturity without help. Someone watched over them. The bushes did not survive by accident.

Their location was not due to a simple spur-of-the-moment decision. That had been determined sometime before. Grandfather Olaf and Grandmother Anna arranged for burial in that spot. They laid to rest Anna's mother, Brita Stina Jonsdotter. Following that, in the same time frame, they also buried two other family members.

They chose the burial spot nearby, because Anna could go there to weep her tears of farewell. She could go there to put a jar of violets on the grave in springtime. She could go there to remember loved ones who had left her care.

They chose the burial spot nearby, because there was no burying ground for the members of Knife Lake Baptist Church. Probably, Olaf and Anna could have buried their departed ones in the Lutheran Cemetery located a half mile south of the farm, but they preferred not to. Maybe they were not far enough removed from the dominion of the State Church in Sweden from which they had emigrated.

During the time I walked near the bushes, pausing now and then to touch a leaf or listen for the faint whispering of the wind through the boughs, I wished I had known exactly when they had been planted. We will never know.

Never know when Great-Grandmother Brita Stina Jonsdotter sighed and laid her head down to its final resting place. That much is left to the clouds that cover the past. There are no markers except for the three bushes to note their passing.

Outsiders view those lilacs with curiosity. But theirs is an idle curiosity. The same curiosity that brushes past grave markers in a cemetery, pausing once in a while to quote a name, a date, or an epitaph.

The lilac bushes are a living epitaph. "Anna and Olaf laid their loved ones here," it says. "They have gone to be with their Maker. When did they die? Well, time, after all is a fabrication of living humanity."

I'm glad I walked in bare feet many times beside those lilac bushes. I'm glad that I seemed to hear voices in the soft winds that stroked the grasses growing near their graves. That I not only know the location of the place, but I know too, the smells, the feeling of the bushes' leaves and the serenity found there.

They blended so well into the landscape that I did not see them apart from the surroundings anymore than I saw the big rock that was left in the field since it was too heavy to move. I did not see the bushes singly anymore than I saw, as a separate feature, the gravelly patch at the curve of the river that we called, "The Washout."

The bushes were full grown at the time I first knew them. When their leaves dropped in the fall of the year, the branches looked gnarled and bony. When the new growth came during spring, stubs of green peppered the bare boughs with their promise of sprouting leaves and the buds that promised pyramiding clusters of lavender blossoms.

I studied the bushes sometimes, intrigued by the fact that they had been planted to be a memorial. Once they had viewed the wagon traffic on the road a few yards away and heard the teamster clucking to his horses "So-o-o Prince, Giddyap Blackie!" They had heard the gravel swishing against metal rims of the wagon wheels.

The bushes were there before men came to dig holes in the ground and place huge poles into those holes. Before men strung wires from one pole to another. Magical wires transmitting voices from one place to another. Wires that connected the poles to funny-looking boxes on the walls of houses. Wires that hooked people up with other people miles away.

The bushes stood rigidly still one day when a shadow passed over them. No, it was not a cloud passing over the sun. It was a swiftly moving shadow. After a few minutes, it passed again, and the bushes shuddered as with a ghostly passing. They had survived to this time when an airplane moved through the skies.

Sometimes, people had walked along the road near the lilac bushes. "Look at that," a woman said one day to the man who walked with her. "Lilac bushes planted in the middle of the field. Isn't that strange?"

The two stopped then, and the man turned his video camera on the lilac bushes "We want proof of this," he said. He focused his camera on the bushes after checking the distance and the light.

The bushes waited for something to happen. Nothing did. The man and woman walked on to take pictures of something else. The bushes were on film. No one could ever deny their presence.

§§§

thirty four

THE PANSY BED

From the kitchen window, she could see
Their pansy faces dipping flippantly.

We all suffered through the drought in the 1930's. Some who had been prosperous, lost crops and livestock and, likewise their prosperity. Some lost interest in their farms as they watched a hay crop harvest at one-half its usual yield. And some lost hope.

You could understand only if you lived through it. We watched the western sky for signs of a cloud that might increase in size until it dropped a deluge of rain. The merciless heat dragged on, temperatures in the upper 90's day after day.

People reacted differently. My mother looked for something to heal the spirit. One day, with plenty of hard work gnawing at the hours, she began a project.

I had no idea what she was going to do when she approached the northern limits of our yard with spade and hoe. Overhead, the sun beat down mercilessly as it had done since early spring. Hardly a breath of air stirred. The only evidence of life was the soft "Who-whoo-whooo" of mourning doves calling from branches of the trees.

Mama aimed her spade at the hard packed clay surface. It was virgin soil. When she managed to dig out a chunk of earth, she had to separate the network of tangled roots. As she thrust the spade into the ground time after time, she reached out now and then to crumble the clods with her hands. Then, she could shake off the dirt and toss the lifeless grass aside.

It was a slow process, but her progress became clear as the hot afternoon hours moved on. What had been a square of turned earth about twelve inches wide doubled, then tripled in size. Mama stopped several times to refresh herself with water in a covered fruit jar. I could see bubbles on the inside of the glass, which meant the water temperature had risen with the heat of the sun. Still, it slaked her thirst.

I looked up to see spirals of dust spinning across the farmyard and along the driveway. They hugged themselves with their spectral arms and danced along at a fiendish tempo. I felt heartsick watching for I knew they were dust devils, another evidence of the dry, dusty conditions of the land.

I sought my refuge, a half-hidden place beneath the poplar trees that I considered my playroom. A rock held down some scraps of paper I had left there. The surface of each was covered with my scrawled words, original verses that satisfied the hunger of my soul. I could hardly find room on the paper scraps to write anything. Yet, the paper was precious to me because I could erase some of the markings and have nearly fresh paper again.

A pine tree in the yard traced its shadow eastward across the lawn before I looked up again. Once more, I anchored my paper and went to check on Mama.

Now, her diggings had become a real flowerbed. I could hardly believe my eyes. After smoothing the surface, Mama had planted her pansy seeds. I had seen them, and I wondered how such funny-looking seeds could produce anything.

The garden stood finished except for one important thing. A few feet beyond its limits stood the shed housing the pump. Mama went there to pump by hand pail after pail of water. She came back and sprinkled it over the flowerbed being careful not to disturb the dust over the seeds.

Her flowers showed up as rows of wet earth in the middle of the clay dust. The pattern left there had the appearance of ancient hieroglyphics.

Somehow through the procession of hot days that promised rain but produced none, Mama's pansies emerged, While gardeners often plant pansy seedlings, she had planted the seeds. No day was too hot or too busy for Mama to water her garden treasures. I realized now that she planted them in that place with a purpose.

And inevitably, the day arrived when the pansies bloomed. The plot was resplendent in color - - yellow, purple, inky-blue and sky-blue. How proud I felt the day a car stopped in the road. A man and woman came walking up to the house, and Mama went to meet them. They were strangers who introduced themselves - - The Hansons from over Brookpark way.

"We came to look at your beautiful flowers," the man said. I saw the blush creep over Mama's cheeks. I watched her smile that lit up the gaunt hollows in her face.

When the visitors left, Mama sent a bouquet with them. She wrapped the stems in a piece of wet cloth so the flowers wouldn't wilt. She picked them tenderly, and parted with them reluctantly.

Through the long hot days that left browned grass in their passing, we feasted hungry eyes on the pansies. A small breeze was all it took to make the pansies turn their heads. If I happened to walk beside the bed, I could see that they nodded at me. I nodded in return.

When the kitchen became an inferno with the cook stove blasting out heat, I noticed that Mama looked outside often. She smiled each time and I knew she liked the sight of pansy faces turned upward.

§§§

thirty five
THE POPLAR GROVE

With every romping breeze that came to play,
The poplar leaves spun briskly night or day.

The row of poplars had stood there as long as I could remember. "Popples," they were called. They stood close enough together for their branches to entwine. I used to wonder if the wrens nesting there would forget which one was home.

Poplars are not highly regarded as trees, because their wood is soft. Also, they grow fast, but do not live to be very old. Family legend has it that the grove was planted during a time of drought. Poplars are probably one of the few kinds of trees that could survive under those conditions.

No doubt, Grandfather Olaf would have been shocked to learn that the trees did not survive him by many years. One by one they became victims of disease. Once started, the grove diminished at a rapid rate.

Even during my childhood, growths had begun to develop along their trunks that warned of trouble ahead.

Even so, I envied those trees because they could look out over the countryside and see a long ways. Whenever I looked out through the upstairs window, I had a better view, too, but I felt convinced that the poplars had the best view of all.

I liked the poplar trees' lively chatter. "We're having a good time," they seemed to say. Their hard leaves hanging suspended on long stems allowed them to swing this way and that. It was especially interesting to see the leaves' silvery undersides. They looked like the inside of my winter coat lining.

If the silvery undersides showed freely, Papa announced, "The wind is in the east. Those silvery leaves are like a weather vane. There's going to be a change."

I waited until no one was nearby to notice me. When I could escape attention, I went outside to check again. Shivers went up my spine when I watched as the leaves danced and spun in the wind. Sure enough, the leaves whirled around, and around, leaving their undersides open to view.

When the wind came up, the leaves clattered, noisily. It sounded to me as if they had a story to tell but no one heard them. Maybe they told of "life" in the poplars.

About squirrels shimmying up and down over the rough-barked exterior, learning everyone's secrets. About the mother squirrel who gave birth to ten offspring. About the sentinel squirrel who dispatched messages if their lives were in danger. About a certain hawk seen flying low in their territory.

For whatever reason the poplars were planted, they served one clear purpose. It was to provide a backing against which our wood was piled. Chunks sawed into lengths for the cook stove and the living room heater had a designated place.

At the poplars' feet, in an area unmolested by lawn mowers or other destructive contrivances, our bed of rhubarb plants prospered. Homely and despised as they were, we relied on them for Mama's unexcelled rhubarb preserves rich with orange and lemon peel.

From an impractical point of view - - which suited my child's devotion to dreams - - I saw the rhubarb as umbrellas to protect the elves. They offered refuge from a blazing sun in July and a shelter from rain and hail storms. The elves' kindly monarch, I pretended, gave such privileges to his subjects. There could be no favoritism in his kingdom.

As for the poplars themselves, I viewed the trees as my own for various purposes. One purpose was private and secretive. "If you vault your dreams from a high place," I pretended, "they will fly higher." I vaulted as many dreams as I dared standing on an upended chunk of poplar, while someone in the kitchen waited for the wood I was sent to bring.

It was hard to tell which trees the birds nested in. I only knew that a song sparrow sang from the branches of the poplars. He sang like a concert artist, blind for the moment to such dangers as the hovering hawk. He sang without need for applause or compliments.

The poplar grove supplied a good windbreak. It was true, however, that most of our prevailing winds came from the north and west. Grandfather Olaf may have planted trees on the east side of the house in a mood of indulgence.

And maybe he, too, listened for the music of the leaves when the wind blew.

The woodpile set up against the poplar grove proved to be the setting for an unforgettable incident. Several of us gathered near the back door of the house one day. Our attention was drawn toward the grove.

A mother woodchuck came out of seclusion in her home beside the poplars. She looked each way, very carefully. Fortunately, the dog, Hero, had found better things to do that afternoon. And, we were partially hidden by a corner of the screen porch.

The mother woodchuck paused and waddled away, followed by one, two, three, four, five little woodchucks. They headed for the barn and outbuildings. The poplars looked on, impassively.

The sun was still high in the late afternoon. Each woodchuck produced a chunky-looking shadow that moved solemnly toward some distant destination. Their act was well planned, not one offspring stepped out of place.

The slow, studied pace of their procession indicated that they knew where they were bound and why. Apparently, the babies could hear their mother's orders, even though we could not hear.

Until this time of release, the popple trees and woodpile had harbored them.

While not the stateliest of trees, the poplars furnished shade from the sun on a day that promised blistering heat. When the sun's position moved westerly, the poplars seemed to pull their branches inward to furnish whatever shade they could for all that lived in the hospitality of that realm.

When the breezes stirred the hard-surfaced leaves on the poplars, they made a rhythmic noise like castanets. They exchanged silence for an enlivened background of sound. It provided a suitable accompaniment for bird songs.

The wood of the poplars was spurned, chiefly because it was soft and spongy. Chunks of poplar branches lopped off for disease or because they were maimed became fuel only when there was nothing else in the woodpile.

When I was a small child, I discovered I could find knots and holes in the poplars. There I planted my own crop of whimsies. A tiny, folded up poem just fit into the hole in a poplar tree. Sometimes it would disappear. I suffered agonies then, wondering if someone in the family had found it. More than likely a bird used it to insulate its nest.

It is hard to say what Grandfather Olaf would have thought about that. But, a man who dreamed a home in America with enough land for a church knew dreams first hand. Surely, he would not have laughed at mine.

§§§

thirty six
THE PINE TREE

Towering above us, that pine tree
Stood in our yard for half a century.

A tall stalwart pine tree dominated the yard, marking the northern limits of our home place. Its height and girth provoked many comments. Interested persons would sometimes ask "Is it ancient?"

That was hardly possible since most of the trees in our area were second growth. Logging operations had cleared out the greater part of our first growth timber sometime during the Nineteenth Century.

While the O'Neal Logging Company, the largest one in our area, may not have logged off the place where our farm was located, there were many smaller companies logging those acres, too.

As for the pine tree in our yard, I feel sure that Grandfather Olaf Norberg had been the planter. I can picture him digging the hole, placing the tree in that opening, and then tucking it in, firmly. Maybe he drove sticks into the ground around the spot so the tree would not be harmed.

Most likely, he gave the tree a drink of water once in a while. Grandmother Anna, watching him, probably shook her head, "My, how he likes that tree," she probably said (in Swedish) with a smile.

When it grew to an uneven shape, he pruned it. And, then, he probably felt proud to watch it grow straighter. He fussed over it the way a mother fusses over her child. After it rose higher than the house chimney, more than likely, he thought it was strong enough to last as long as the house.

Because if its location we saw more of that tree than any other. The maple on the opposite side of the house towered over lilacs and honeysuckle bushes. But, otherwise, kept to itself. The massive willow tree, beside the road, on whose bough we had our swing, murmured summer songs but was content to keep its place. The poplars marching across the eastern boundary of our yard maintained a stiff resistance to any dangers in that direction but did not challenge the pine tree's being the King of the Yard.

The latter, shaped so perfectly, hovered over us like a kindly giant. It saw that we had a lawn covering of pine cones. It protected us from north winds. It spread wide branches over the duff piled up underneath. I, for one, liked that because we didn't have to mow there.

Further, the tree caught the attention of people passing by. Often, they stopped to comment on the tree's size and beauty. It was a king of trees. We counted on its strength   but, we learned, even a king is not safe from disaster.

A storm struck one night. It came out of the west, hurling its anger at us. Torrents of rain slashed the house. Thunder roared so loudly it seemed to drown out our thoughts.

Then, we heard a dreadful, crashing noise, followed by thunder that sounded like the high point in the musical production performed by our town's band.

When morning came we saw the damage. Lightning had struck the pine tree. It lay, helpless, across our lawn, its top not far from the kitchen window.

Where the trunk broke, after the strike, great splinters lay open to view. Once, I had heard the splinters from fallen trees were giants' toothpicks. I wonder if I would see the giants come to get them if I stayed up all night. It was an awful thought. It made me shiver.

Neighbors stopped in to see the damage and swap storm damage stories. I felt sensitive about having them stand around, talking about our tree. *What if it could hear?*

It was my first experience with loss of any kind. I learned that if I went out of the house via the back door, I didn't need to see the fallen pine. If I didn't see it, I didn't have that sick feeling in my stomach.

Papa and a helper sawed the tree from its trunk. I stayed in a room where I could not see the activity. The chunks were hauled away to a separate pile from the one stacked beside the poplars. Left alone there, they could dry out and age.

We used the pine's loss for a reference to time. Someone in the family might say "Oh, that happened just before the pine tree was struck down!" Or, "I remember now, it was just after the pine tree fell." Or "Yes, that happened the same year we lost the pine tree."

As for me, I liked the tree but I had complained about it too. I remember saying "Mama, I can't see the North Star from here. That old tree is in the way."

Those were words I wished I hadn't spoken. Life was teaching me a lesson in recognizing what really matters. As once the tree may have been pruned to guide its growth, I was being pruned in my growth, too.

The tree lines on in memory. I think of it as on a summer night when fireflies trimmed its dark green branches. I remember the silky spider webs caught among the pine needles. I picture it as shivering but enjoying the rain that fell in a shower on a warm July day.

I remember its loftiness when an early snowfall flocked its branches. It seemed to hug to itself the majestic white covering draped around the tree. It looked like it belonged in a noble scene where the great king pulled his robes around him and posed for the picture an artist was painting.

The tree was a mighty presence in our lives. It seems as real today in memory as it stood in reality. It has never quite disappeared into the past.

§§§

thirty seven

THE DUMPING GROUND

Today's belongings are tomorrow's trash,
Will usefulness and fond attachment clash?

I walked through the pastureland with nothing more in mind than listening to the river's voice or checking on the dragonflies in the marshy places. But, I stopped abruptly. In the place where the river curved, the shore was gravelly. There to my horror, I found our old organ that I loved so much.

Once it stood in the living room. But mute keys and a wheezy tone had dulled its favor. It had been replaced by a piano considered better but of equally ancient vintage.

The organ, for a while, resided on the landing to the second floor. With sobs in my throat and tears in my eyes, I played it there. Stubbornly, I refused to accept its demise.

Now, I found it almost submerged in water at a place we called "The Washout." For years this had been our dumping ground. Enough water sluiced through the place to wash debris down-river.

But, my beloved organ was still alive to me. When I bent to play a chord, I found the keys were silent. Minnows swam among the black and white keys like dark moods looking for shadows in which to hide.

My dreams vanished. *Life was cruel if it allowed destruction of things we love! How could I trust anything now?*

We gave no thought to pollution. Our community believed in the supreme rights of the property holder. We trusted the habits built up through the years. "Why, it's all right," we might say. "We've always done it this way."

All I could think of was that wonderful old organ with water eroding its value. Perhaps subterranean creatures would find a home in its recesses. I leaned down to listen for even a whisper, but all I heard was a sleepy clucking noise like the chickens made when they were getting ready for the night.

For some time, I stayed away from that part of the river. I did not even visit the dragonflies in their marshy places where water lilies floated on the river's surface like frosted cakes dancing along, decorating a party dream.

Sadly, I skirted those areas and moved on to the deeper places. The music of the water was richer there and more varied. When I stood on the knoll nearby, I could see my reflection in the water. I pretended it was a nymph and my twin. It looked exactly like me.

There, I saw the biggest turtle I had ever seen. It emerged from the water, and climbed on the bank. It lumbered along slowly, sometimes showing its head, and at other times, headless. I was too much in awe of it to even pretend that it wanted me for a friend.

Here the density of the undergrowth increased. Just beyond the next curve the two rivers met - - The Knife River flowing out of Knife Lake and the Snake River circling the town of Mora.

We were forbidden to go to that place. The prospect of danger made visiting it more desirable, but I was unwilling to forfeit my rambling privileges for one quick glance at the rivers coming together. Instead I pretended that a Fairy Princess lived in the area. She wanted complete privacy, and forbade anyone to enter uninvited.

I wandered along the course I had taken. My plan was to skirt the washout where the organ lay, but I could not resist another look. I leaned down as far as possible to hear what the rippling waters said. All I heard was a gurgling sound. It made me think of when I listened at the hollow of the old oak tree...all I heard was my own breathing.

Comforted, then, I returned home. While my heart still felt heavy, I could think about the organ without crying.

I felt a forgiving tolerance for everyone. All the same, I looked at everything I loved with a concerned eye. *When would they haul away the library table from the living room? The dresser in Mama and Papa's bedroom on which stood the milk glass dish that had a setting hen on its cover?*

Some of my dreams and ideals lay in The Washout, drowned like the music from our beloved organ.

§§§

thirty eight

THE FENCE POSTS

They strutted by the roadside up and down
Some heading north and others toward the town

I knew the fence lines of our property well. They were, in fact, our property lines. They had been surveyed in Grandfather Olaf's time by surveyors for Knife Lake Township, Kanabec County, Minnesota, and they were never changed.

Some people said they felt closed in by the fences. I felt surprised to hear that, because I found them comforting. They had put their stamp on the legal description of the acreage. They determined what belonged to us. They kept out intruders. And, they gave us a sense of privacy - - Maybe an exaggerated sense of privacy.

Barbed wire fences, to be sure, leave a place open to view. Most of our fence posts carried three lengths of barbed wire. The only places holding more were areas where extra strain might result from keeping animals in or out, as the case may be.

I had been taught to report any fence breakdown I saw, after which Papa set out to fix the places that had weakened, no longer providing barriers to the escape of animals. We must not let the milk cows get free.

While some of our neighbors had metal fence posts, ours were rough-hewn from felled trees on our farm. The bark was still on them, and the inner surface was cut with an axe, leaving long jagged splinters on the raw wood. The latter fascinated me, because I could hear the ring of the axe that split them.

The latter, in fact, was what I liked most about our fences. Since the wooden posts were taken from trees on our farm, I felt close to them. I felt they had a right to be there as much as I did. Fenceposts that had been discarded were split up into wood for the stoves. They were still in use on our farm - - Grandfather Olaf's farm. It was part of the system that allowed us to be landowners. And as such, we needed fences.

Our young but well-trained eyes could spot weaknesses in the fences quite easily. They were of personal concern to me because I was often being chased by an irate mother cow who became aroused by maternal instincts. At such times, she might become mean-spirited.

In the act of bringing the cows home to milk, I often had to run for my life with the newest mother cow in pursuit. And not far enough behind for my comfort.

With an eye for that, I assessed the conditions of the fences quite regularly. I put in a request for fence work wherever there was a problem. While that seems a lot of responsibility for a child, no doubt, in a few days I would have occasion to test the condition of the fences again - - at risk of my life.

I became quite agile, and found that I could run like a deer and slip between the wires in a few seconds. It was not at all unusual for me to come home from this chore with barbed wire scratches on my arms and legs, and considerable harm done to my sense of security.

Most of my chores brought me near the river to which I felt drawn. And, also, I liked to run downhill toward the river with the wind at my back. My skirts puffed up like balloons and I felt free from care.

As for the fenceposts, they paraded around from spring to fall to winter and then spring again. They kept their places in good weather and in bad. They occasionally broke down when a neighbor's unruly animal jumped the wires and dragged the posts to the ground.

When that happened, we turned out as a family. It was, in fact, quite a hullabaloo. We ran and yelled and sicked the dog to show our authority. There was no system to our efforts to get rid of the runaway cow and bring order back to our premises.

But there was a lot of activity. Even when the weather was bad, we enjoyed it because it was a departure from our ordinary routine. That routine which sometimes became all too full of sameness.

In the end, when the neighbor came after his escapee cow, we visited with him and showed friendliness. If he ever guessed that we had sicked the dog on him as part of the game, neither he, nor we ever let on.

It was all part of the ritual on a place where fences kept some creatures in and some out. We were not guilty of a real crime. It was just that sometimes we needed to help our neighbors and friends treat us to merriment. In return for that, we put on our family act. Harmless enough, and our right as property owners. Property owners, in fact, with fenced in acreage.

§§§

thirty nine
THE OLD BARN

In stanchions side-by-side the cattle stood,
The milk they gave was for our livelihood

Built of logs, the main wing of the old barn seemed to crouch down to the level of its doorway. Grandfather Olaf must not have been very tall. But, Papa ducked every time he went through the doorway.

Wind whistling through cracks in the adjacent haymow greeted anyone who entered. It had a plaintive sound like lost children or puppies taken from their mother too soon.

The stanchions, made of wood, met over the cow's head in a sort of yoke that clasped together. Those yokes, rickety and insecure, came undone all too easily. When that happened, the cow that was getting personal attention at the moment walked away, leaving the milker with a partially filled mail of milk and with fingers poised for the next pull-and-squeeze operation.

Just beyond the milking area the calf-pen held all the latest additions. Whenever a cow got loose from its insecure fastenings, it walked over to the pen. Maybe in the scene that followed she found her calf of fairly recent weeks.

It might be a noisy reunion, but it did not last long. The two of them, cow and calf, became bored in a short time, and then they parted company again. The cow wandered away to see if she could find anything of more lasting interest. Usually she gave up and returned so the milking could go on.

During the winter months, most of the barn work was done by light from lanterns. Their flickering, uneasy light threw strange, shifting patterns against the walls. I always expected doors to slam and the lanterns to snuff out.

The old barn offered shelter to a lot of cats. They continually produced tawny colored kittens that begged for milk and fought among themselves for the right to patrol the length and width of the barn for mice. The yowls of hungry kittens surmounted any other sounds.

Occasionally, one cat would emerge from the number lodging there as a sort of pet. One less wild than the others. One that rubbed against my leg, begging for attention. One that I might call Tiger or Calico or Puss of the Barn Kingdom.

That one rose to a position of its own. Still, just one of the barn cats, certainly not a rival of Mama's pet hen, Dumpling. The latter followed Mama right to the doorway of the house. At least until she disappeared, leaving nothing behind but a pile of feathers and a decided skunk odor.

Windows of the barn were the original ones installed when the barn was new. They appeared to have sunk into their places. Spider webs covered every inch of space available. Those webs held flies as prisoners. Although I disliked flies, I felt sad to see how they fluttered helplessly in their prisons.

Along the outside walls of the barn, big hooks provided places for hanging things. Lengths of chain looking important and practical, hung there.

Papa hung the bridles and harnesses for the horses on that wall, but, in spite of his neatness, stray pieces of rope appeared, too, as well as clumps of twine, and even a pail, hung by its handle.

Surprising things turned up on those hooks in the barn. A pair of Papa's suspenders, for example and once, even one of Mama's crocheted potholders. An apron of Mama's, its printed pattern faded and covered with grime hung there looking lost and out of place.

The combs Papa used for currying the horses and the scissors for trimming their manes and tails hung on hooks.

The leather items became shrunken and shabby. Sometimes, though, Papa took out a container of some kind of oil and daubed it on the leather items. The oil had a pungent smell that cut through all the other odors and hung in the air for a day or so - - a sharp, clean smell.

Papa continued to harvest such things as hay to put in the haymow. The old barn played its part. By that time, the haymow stood empty. The day came when the big door to the hayloft stood open.

A second crop of hay filled the hayrack, and all of it would go inside. The haymow, the barn, and the whole yard became fragrant with the smell of the new mown hay. A fragrance of clover and wild flowers filled every crack of the old barn. Riches of the countryside breathed from every pore of the building. The perfume combined hints of ripening apples on trees in the countryside with herbs, both tame and wild, as well as grapes hanging over the fences along roads.

Then, Papa began thinking seriously about meeting the demands through the winter season. During years of normal rainfall, the hay meadows and alfalfa supplied enough hay for winter storage, but those conditions did not always exist on our farm. At such a time, he took the scythe down from its place on one wall of the granary. The scythe, a piece of equipment with a long curved blade, looked as vicious as it was useful. The curve assisted in adjusting to the uneven surface as its cutting edge swept along the ground.

Papa began by sharpening the blade. Perched on the grinder's seat in the machine shed, he held the blade against the concrete surface of the grinder. The wailing sound of that operation shut out any other noise.

A pail of water stood nearby so that Papa could keep the concrete surface moistened. If it dried off, sparks flew. I thought they looked like star showers on a summer night.

One small patch of grass did not yield much hay, but the total amount   from several of the patches "counted up."

When I read the Bible story about Ruth gleaning left-over sheaves of grain behind the harvesters, I felt I knew the nature of that work. Taking hay from a ditch or from patches at the ends of fields close to the fence posts, seemed to be of the same nature.

If Papa looked behind him when he hand-raked, he stopped to pick up every blade of grass or wild grain behind the scythe. I tried to do the same thing but discovered it requires a special skill.

Sometimes, thistle sprouted among the wild grain and grasses. Papa tossed out those offenders. A farmer could not afford to bring along such wasteful stuff.

Sometimes, the bees attracted to stands of sweet clover kept up a menacing chorus nearby. At such times I didn't go near even big colorful clover blossoms. Laws of the countryside are simple but demanding. If you observe them, you seldom get hurt.

The old barn brought comments from passersby. *When was it built? Were we going to build a new one?*

That took place more quickly than we had expected through one of the farm programs of President Roosevelt's New Deal. To Papa's great joy, he found himself with a new hip-roofed barn that was finished in the fall of the year.

Sometime later, I looked out one evening to see a big, trembling orange harvest moon that appeared to be caught on the hay sling cable from the haymow's open door.

The sight almost made me forget my grief over seeing the old building abandoned in the shadow of the new barn.

§§§

forty

THE CHOICE

My choice of breed is bound to be the best,
It will put your make or model to the test.

I confess to having gotten no warm, fuzzy feelings from being near cows. They were creatures that served a need. It did seem to me like a miracle that the grass and other edibles they consumed - - when digested - - came out of these creatures in the form of milk.

Still, cows were just cows as far as I was concerned. I left it to others to determine which were the best makes or models. How they measured up against each other did not concern me in the least.

I knew those rivalries were present. Of all the disputes, I think the Guernsey/Holstein was the liveliest.

In spite of those disputes, we were peace-loving people. Our feuds were never on a par with the Hatfields and McCoys - - those hill people who feuded among themselves for months and even years.

No, our feuds were more on par with friendly competition. Our neighbors who in time became the proud owners of an Allis-Chalmers tractor swore there was nothing like it. Down the road a few miles another neighbor bought a McCormick-Deering.

The latter bought his at the time of the county fair. He drove away with it, waving to the neighbors and doffing his wide-brimmed straw hat. He might have been a beauty queen greeting her throngs of admirers.

As to performance, the Allis-Chalmers vs. McCormack-Deering controversy was long-lasting. It went on as long as I can remember. The two pieces of equipment became lost in the years. Only the names remained.

I remember that contest fondly. It was as good as the Leghorn vs. Rhode Island (chicken) contest. Owners of the latter proclaimed them to be better "layers" than the Leghorns. If the chickens were to be used for eating purposes though, the Leghorns were said to be, by far, tastier than the Rhode Island Reds.

As for the Guernsey vs. Holsteins, every owner came up with a different story. In a mixed herd, it was almost always the Guernsey that became the bell cow. The latter was the cow that took lead position among the herd. Usually, a bell was hung around her neck. She was the first one moving down the lane toward home in the evening. The other cows followed, one by one. They made a red-and-white spattered parade, dear to a farmer's heart.

Some rivalries are unhealthy. But not so the Guernsey vs. Holstein issue. "Mine's better than yours!" was the gist of the contest. Neither side hoped to be proven right. It just made farming a little more interesting to have such a rivalry going.

Of course, we must use reason in all matters. Tempers might become a little testy if we got into the Lutheran vs. Baptist issue or the Democrat vs. Republican.

Some matters are too sensitive to be discussed. It is best that we keep focused on whatever is least sensitive to us. In our case, we'll keep our red-and-white Guernseys and you keep your black-and-white Holsteins.

§§§

forty one

THE GARDEN

The garden is a sundial if you read it right,
Its shifting shadows tell you when the day is taking flight.

The garden lay stretched out under the strong spring sun. It was like a tigress that welcomes her young to feed from her strength. The garden patch dreamed of giving a rich yield.

We, the farmers, knew every inch of that piece of earth. We had run garden cultivators, and we had raked the clay clods out of our path. We had tossed away stones, although more continued to surface - - our legacy from the glaciers that passed this way thousands of years before the garden existed.

We spread the fertilizer. We looked at the garden patch's nakedness and wondered how we could believe that it would yield much of anything. It was hard to remember what we had reaped from it in former years.

The space just south of our house measured, roughly, fifty by eighty feet. From the moment we marked the rows, we began expecting bushels of produce. We dreamed into the existence the tender vegetables that would thrive there and that we would take from this fertile earth.

Robins chirped exultantly as we worked the garden, hopping about, feasting on earthworms and insects brought to the surface by the cultivating and raking and hoeing. They feasted on beetles and grubs that enriched the soil where they lived. The heavy soil of this garden patch held moisture for a long time. It cradled in its composition the hopes for many a meal.

When, at last, preparations were completed, the garden patch lay ready and waiting for the rain and sun to perform their magic. We had done our part. We could only wait for things to happen.

As the tiny plants emerged, they became strangled by weeds. I grieved over the carrots. Fragile little lacy sprouts appeared above the earth only to be surrounded by ragweeds that dwarfed and ran over them.

In other instances, I noted the weeds that appeared which strongly resembled the plant itself - - Sometimes called "fool's gold."

Onions seemed to spring out of the garden after planting, ready for use in a few days' time. Peas emerged pale and dainty while beans sprouted with a look that meant business. Blossoms, and then long pods ready for the table.

Once begun, the race was on. The plants grew with such revelry, they outdistanced one another, seeking the good graces of the sun and preening under the touch of raindrops.

Raindrops all too scant during the drought years. How the plants shrank under the scorching sun! How they seemed to gasp for breath and wilt when no relief came!

We carried hand-pumped water to the garden. That saved some of the plants, but the vegetables drooped in the heat, the plants appeared listless-looking and frail. The small amount of water we had was no match for the relentless power of the sun as our country grappled with its erosion problem in the western plains. Perhaps the best reason for carrying water to the plants was to relieve our helpless feelings.

As the garden developed, sometimes peapods appeared but the peas themselves had shrunk to nothing. Pale beans hung limply to vines. Every meal we served from those vegetables was an apology.

We watched over our vegetables carefully, for they were our hope of food for the winter months. Cabbage plants had real endurance, and we encouraged them in their growth although none of us cared much for cabbage. We banked all our hopes on the tomato crop and, possibly, corn to can.

In years before we had had our shelves in the cellar lined with peas and beans, with beets and carrots. The supply on those shelves had become slim. It was frightening to see what the drought had done to our food supply. A late spring shower had prompted us to plant some late vegetables. If those fared better than the early crop, we would have them for canning and preserving.

During normal years of rainfall the garden fed us well.

The patch of earth just east of the house was reserved for strawberries. That plot sagged down low. Water drained into the patch from adjoining areas, and that kept the soil moist. It was an ideal spot for strawberries.

One poor rabbit who ventured forth to taste those red-ripe berries met with an unfortunate incident. Mama, moved to unusually severe tactics because of the stress of the drought years, threw her broom at the rabbit as he was sampling those delicacies for breakfast. Caught unawares, he fell down. When he got up, again, he appeared stunned, but, Mama, unrepentant, merely brandished her broom once more to frighten the rabbit away.

Such items as cucumbers and squash were planted toward the fringes of the garden. The produce, like wayfarers, wandered some distance to the east and south. These plants, later in their growth and fruition, escaped our watchful eyes.

We were worn down, in good years by the labor of picking produce and getting it ready for preservation. During the dog days of August, we moved much more slowly and were apt to overlook a cucumber growing in shade under the big leaves of the plant.

And, thus, some of our vegetables were not prevented from leaving home. When I struck off across the field toward the pasture to get the cows, I might find cucumbers lurking in the long grass beyond the limits of our dooryard. Sometimes those cucumbers had ripened. They were big - - eight inches wide - - and we didn't want to eat them. The inside was full of seedy pulp. They had lost their ability to become pickles.

Then they became food for the hogs that squealed their delight - - to my disgust. Putting them to good use was part of the philosophy of life in the farm picture. "That's what you get for leaving home," I told those big awkward cucumbers and toppled them heartlessly into the pigpen.

The squash were even greater wanderers. Their dark skins made it easier for them to hide in the tall grass. They might ramble southward from the garden patch or east. They hid in the wild grass that grew almost waist-high along untended areas. Free, then, to develop as they wished, some of them became huge. Developing in size did not hurt them for eating.

Many of them were not found until late fall. Then we skirmished around, looking for lost vegetables.

We packed them away in bins in the cellar where they furnished good eating far into the winter. Almost any meal was improved by the appearance of baked squash. The color of gold is always inviting, and, besides, the squash had a robust flavor.

So, it was that we gathered our produce at the end of summer. We were onto their tricks. They couldn't hide from us, usually. I always thought it was fun to find a big squash that had wandered out into the cornfield. The leaves of the corn plants had talked to it, and it seemed to have a richer-than-ever taste.

The time came for the garden to be put to sleep for the winter months. It had held conversation with the butterflies that came to call. It had made friends with the caterpillars that moseyed up and down its paths. It had fraternized with the ants that patrolled its long rows looking for harmful insects.

It had spoken with the spiders that left their dainty webs here and there throughout the garden. We might not notice them until they cupped a dewdrop that caught the rays of the sun. Diamonds in the garden!

After all that, the garden was ready to sleep.

§§§

forty two

THE REPAIRMAN

With best of intentions and a willing hand,
Papa *impaired* machinery in his command.

One of those *delicate* matters which one mentioned only with diplomacy, was that our Papa was not *"mechanically inclined."* That was a phrase bandied about in our neighborhood. A man either was or he wasn't. The statement was both an affirmation and a condemnation, depending on the way you used it. With respect to our Papa, it was often inclined to be more of a condemnation.

When a piece of machinery broke down, we shuddered, collectively. If I should happen to bring Papa water in the field, and thus be present when a breakdown occurred, I might be dispatched to fetch a hammer, a pair of pliers or a wrench.

Sometimes, Papa knew the nature of the breakdown. All he needed was a few tools to remove a part so that it could be taken into Mora to get a replacement. Of course, our machinery was old and removal of a part might mean that you were dealing with rust. That made the job more difficult.

Papa knew the places in Mora that could supply parts and what his chances were of getting the right part. Our machinery was simple and, thus, a lot of expertise was not required to remove the part to take it to the repair shop.

Nevertheless, working outside - - probably under a hot sun - - and maybe in an awkward position - - made the procedure of removing a certain part that needed to be replaced far more difficult.

I watched, often making a private decision as to whether a pair of pliers, a hammer or wrench would be needed. Of course, sometimes the situation called for all three. If I happened to bring water to Papa in the once-upon-a-time syrup pail we used for that purpose, I might discover that the breakdown had just occurred and my visit was timely. I ran back home, then, trying to ignore the stinging touches on my flesh as grasshoppers jumped from the long grass and pelted the skin on my legs.

Once at home, I had no trouble finding the tools for they would be neatly put away in Papa's tool bench in the granary. The problem came if I found more than one kind of tool.

Well, which one should I choose - - the long, tapered pliers or the short stubby one most commonly used? The big hammer with its wooden handle worn smooth from use, or the smaller one (which would be easier to carry)? The wrench on top of the tool bench or the one hung by its handle on the wall above the tool bench? I often faltered in my choice and returned to the field to Papa torn by concern about whether or not I had brought the right one.

Then, came the part that centered on whether or not Papa was mechanically *in*-clined. Sometimes, the part he was attempting to remove was rusted so badly, it defied removal. Using the hammer to pound it was futile. The wrench refused to budge the part from its mooring. The pliers fit over the screws well enough but were no match for the layer of rust that held the part snugly in place.

181

At such times, I concerned myself with gathering wildflowers growing along the fences. I cherished the daisies that grew in abundance. Mixed with sweet clover, they made a beautiful bouquet. Sometimes my search turned up wild columbine. I brought those back to Mama with great pride, knowing she admired them as much as I did. Such a bouquet usually included wild asters. Meadowrue added an interesting touch, too.

I searched to my heart's content until I heard Papa calling me back. Then, I must carry whatever parts he had pried loose back to the house while he brought the team of horses.

I felt proud at such times, because I was sure I had performed a real service. Proud, but a little worried too.

Worried because the next step bringing the part into town. Papa knew all the men in town who would be able to supply a part like the one he had removed. We went to one of the stores. But now, a ticklish situation arose.

"You say, Herman, that this part was on the left side of the mower?"

"Yah. Yah," Papa might say uncertainly. Then, one of the men in the store who came over picked it up and examined it.

"I think this came from the right side," he would declare. Papa pushed back the brim of his hat uncertainly. Several men had gathered by that time. They had a conference during which they decided where the part had come from.

Papa, relieved would say, "Yah, yah. That's what I said in the first place."

When the part was paid for, we were ready to go back home.

"Can you get that back on without trouble, Herman?" one of the men might ask.

An awkward pause was likely to follow.

"Well, I'd better be getting back," Papa said, too jovially.

"Uh, Herman, I'm coming out that way in a little while," a man named George said. "Should I stop by and have a look at that part?"

"That would be all right," Papa replied too carelessly.

And, George did that, coming to the rescue as he and others had done for years.

Later, the part was back on the machine and Papa was ready to go back to work again. In the house we breathed a sigh of relief. It was good to live in a community where men who were mechanically *inclined* helped out the people who were not.

As for me, I arranged the bouquet of flowers to put on our supper table. Mama admired all of them, particularly, the sweet clover and columbine.

§§§

forty three
THE BULL CALF

"Be kind to beasts," I've heard the righteous say,
But patience ran beyond its limits on that day.

I disliked the chore of feeding milk to the "young stock." They consisted of calves born that spring and weaned, but still needing mother's milk. The calves were getting big by this time, especially the bulls.

Feeding the animals, on whose heads stubby horns appeared, meant being confronted with their aggressive behavior. When I put a pail of milk in front of one of them, I stood ready to defend myself - - and Mama stood by, ready to help. Each calf had developed a "butting habit" quite natural to it. A few noisy, slobbery drinks of milk and it became ready to butt the pail. I stood ready to ward off showers of milk drops.

Even worse, those young bulls were not satisfied with their share of the milk. As soon as one of them had finished, he looked around for more. He did that by jostling the females. We kept the trough filled, but if the pushing around was too much for one of them, we let it drink from a pail.

One morning, a bull calf had been particularly difficult. He would not allow the other calves to drink without his getting a share of theirs, too. He pushed the other animals out of the way and stood there, daring them to come back. He rammed his head against fenceposts as if to show us his strength. We had run out of patience.

I held the pail while a young heifer drank from it. The bull calf persisted in coming at the pail, spilling portions of milk. He pestered the young heifers, too, shoving and jostling.

At last, Mama ran out of patience. She armed herself with a board she had picked up from a pile nearby. The next time the young bull tried to push a drinker from the pail, Mama raised the board and hit the bull over the head.

Quieted at last, the bull fell to the ground, his front legs spread widely, his eyes rolling backward into his head. Mama and I watched in horror.

Now, Mama and I wondered about the consequences. How would we ever tell Papa? Did Bull Calf's behavior deserve this? Could we have managed him in some other way?

We had poured some milk into a trough in the feeding Lot. The other animals went on, unconcernedly, drinking milk and pushing each other out of the way. They paid no attention to their fallen comrade. A yellow garden moth flew into the lot and landed on the head of the calf still lying on the ground. As if that gave the calf new energy, he tried to stand. We watched, breathlessly.

Poised as if to fly away, the moth came back to light on the calf's head again. It seemed to inject greater resolution into the calf. He put one foot forward, faltered, and then pushed himself upward on all four legs.

He shook his head as if to rid himself of this disturbing occurrence. He bellowed loudly, twice. With renewed vigor, he stepped forward, butted his way to the edge of the trough, which still contained a little milk, and once again, he drank noisily. Mama and I felt drawn together. We alone experienced this. As if a vow were taken, we agreed to silence.

Just before we left the feeding lot, Mama and I caught each others' eye. We began laughing and laughed until we could hardly stop. Now that the danger had passed, we could appreciate the humor in the situation.

As we walked to the house a light breeze fanned leaves of the poplar trees. It stirred a conversation. A wren answered from somewhere in the trees near the house.

A sheep that Papa was raising as kind of an experiment wandered into the yard with her twin lambs. Playfully, they chased each other. With stiffened legs, they jumped up and down like mechanical toys. All this for a love of living.

Bull Calf began rough-housing again, ramming the other calves with his almost-developed horns. He rammed the side of the old barn nearby, seeming to need to impress us with his superior strength.

But, Mama and I knew the real victor for the day. It was Mama driven at last to let Bull Calf know who was boss.

Violence of any kind was not permitted on our farm. Not to the horses, the cows, the pigs, the chickens, the turkey, the geese or the sheep. But Mama and I knew that sometimes we must take a hand where ordinary forces don't work.

Mama claimed the victory with a weather-beaten board peppered by knot holes.

At breakfast I caught Mama's eye. A smile disappeared into her steaming cup of coffee.

§§§

forty four
EPILOGUE

We've reached the final chapter now and I
Will leave you here to read; this is "goodbye."

In writing these chronicles, I take on the role of family spokesperson. If any family members dispute the basis of my impressions, I offer them the challenge of writing the story on their terms.

Writing the book has been a good experience - - in fact, a satisfying experience. I discovered that my harmony with these people grew as I wrote. I found that the persons I wrote about, such as Grandfather Olaf, Grandmother Anna, and Great-Grandmother Brita Stina Jonsdotter, mellowed as I went along. I interpreted that to mean their spirits are at peace and that I had not disrupted anyone's eternal restfulness. In fact, as I continued to write I found myself more and more familiar with those persons whom I had never met in real life. While they do not have "faces," they certainly have human characteristics.

As for Mama and Papa, I hope I have done them justice. I wish to give them their human-ness, to which we are all entitled.

I believe it has been a sort of "getting acquainted" process. I would like to think I convinced someone else to try the same thing. Even if your facts are meager, you will find that stirring in the mix of family fables turns up more material than you might have hoped for.

As people are prone to say these days "go for it."

As one gathers one's family together on paper as well as in real life, one finds a place to fit in.

I selected one quality of life which I believed I had gained from each person, i.e., respect for Papa's habits for orderliness and awareness of other people's well being-ness or lack of it, from Mama's intuitive judgment. If I am mistaken, I hope it's forgivable. Doing this has given me a new sense of belonging.

If some who read this book say "There she goes again - - making believe," I can live with that. I have given my subconscious mind free reign. I find that it seldom gets into the private affairs of others.

As you read "This Side Of Anywhere" please remember that I am sharing with you, the reader, the impressions of life as we lived it on a small farm in central Minnesota. Bear with me if sometimes my facts don't coincide with your knowledge. I'm dealing in impressions more than facts, anyway.

I have been indelibly affected by the bell in the church that stood on our property, as well as by the singing of hymns heard there in church or wafting through open church windows. For the benefit of those today who believe an orchestral production in church replaces hymn-singing, I can testify that orchestral music would have never left the same impression on me as the church bells and the hymn singing by human voices.

Into the depths of our struggles for economic and personal stability came the heaviest possible blow; the untimely death of our Mama. She slipped away from us quickly after a brief but life-robbing illness.

Through the following years, my senses, as well as my intellect, needed to be nurtured. Without knowing he did so, Grandfather Olaf filled my thirstiness with God-reminders. He donated the land for a church and helped to build the congregation that worshipped there.

I shall always be grateful.

§§§

ABOUT THE AUTHOR

Vivian Norberg Loken has written for publication for the past thirty years. She describes herself as having a zestful appetite for living, a lifelong interest in poetry and an endless fascination with words.

She believes that we get out of life only as much as we invest in it.

She intends to follow this book with another that covers the later period in her life.

§§§